THE SAXON SHORE WAY

Books by Alan Sillitoe

Fiction

Saturday Night and Sunday Morning
The Loneliness of the Long Distance Runner
The General
Key to the Door
The Ragman's Daughter
The Death of William Posters
A Tree on Fire
Guzman, Go Home
A Start in Life
Travels in Nihilon
Raw Material
Men, Women and Children
The Flame of Life
The Widower's Son
The Storyteller
The Second Chance
Her Victory

Poetry and Plays

The Rats and Other Poems
A Falling Out of Love and Other Poems
Love in the Environs of Voronezh
Storm and Other Poems
Snow on the North Side of Lucifer
All Citizens are Soldiers (with Ruth Fainlight)
Three Plays

Essays

Mountains and Caverns

Books by Fay Godwin

The Oldest Road: An Exploration of
    the Ridgeway (with J. R. L. Anderson)
The Oil Rush (with Mervyn Jones)
The Drovers Roads of Wales
    (with Shirley Toulson)
Islands (with John Fowles)
Remains of Elmet (with Ted Hughes)
Romney Marsh (with Richard Ingrams)
Tess, the Story of a Guide Dog
    (with Peter Purves)
The Whisky Roads of Scotland
    (with Derek Cooper)
Bison at Chalk Farm

THE SAXON SHORE WAY

FROM GRAVESEND TO RYE

Alan Sillitoe and
Fay Godwin

Hutchinson

London Melbourne Sydney Auckland Johannesburg

Hutchinson & Co. (Publishers) Ltd
An imprint of the Hutchinson Publishing Group
17–21 Conway Street, London W 1 P 6 JD

Hutchinson Group (Australia) Pty Ltd
30–32 Cremorne Street, Richmond South, Victoria 3121
PO Box 151, Broadway, New South Wales 2007

Hutchinson Group (NZ) Ltd
32–34 View Road, PO Box 40–086, Glenfield, Auckland 10

Hutchinson Group (SA) Pty Ltd
PO Box 337, Bergvlei 2012, South Africa

First published 1983
Photographs © Fay Godwin 1983
Text © Alan Sillitoe 1983

Photographs printed by Mervyn Arthur

Set in Monophoto Ehrhardt
by Balding + Mansell Limited, Wisbech, Cambs

Printed in Great Britain by Balding + Mansell Limited, Wisbech, Cambs
and bound by Wm Brendon & Son Ltd, Tiptree, Essex

British Library Cataloguing in Publication Data

Sillitoe, Alan
    The Saxon Shore Way.
    1. Saxon Shore Way   2. South East (England) –
    Description and travel
    I. Title   II. Godwin, Fay
    796.5′1′09422   DA670.S/

ISBN 0 09 151460 6 cased
        0 09 151461 4 Hutchinson Paperback

Front cover: East Cliffs, Dover
Back cover: The Street, Whitstable

The photographs are for Giles Gordon

Contents

The Street, Whitstable

Chapter One
Blame the Saxons

If one looks at England, south and southeast from London, as by the bird's eye view of a topographical map, and imagines it in danger from the encroachment of an enemy, one sees that the coast of Kent forms the exposed left flank of any possible defences. Part of the line is the nearest England comes to a foreign coast, which makes it the most strategically sensitive county in that it has to be traversed by any army before London can be reached. A way around the flank in former times would mean entering the Thames Estuary and braving the guns of Coalhouse Fort on the Essex shore, and those of Cliffe Fort on the Kentish side, with less than one nautical mile between.

Thus, during war, Kent is the exposed outwork of an armed camp, and in times of peace the county has been – and is – the main highway into and out of the country. The shortest sea crossing to the Continent draws armies and travellers to Dover, and sees them come, frequently richer but often none the wiser, home again.

The last attempted invasion of England had the distinction of being the first to be launched by air. As one poet says, or so I heard:

> The coast of Kent is England's chin,
> Jutting out to take the punches;
> The last occasion was
> When German bombers flew in bunches
> To disturb the ploughman's lunches. . . .

Unlike the Norman invasion in 1066 (which took place in Sussex), the attempt at subjugation in 1940 failed, though Kent as a front-line county had over 30,000 high-explosive bombs and threequarters of a million incendiaries unloaded on it, which wrecked or severely damaged more than 20,000 buildings, and caused 21,000 casualties. Much of the Battle of Britain was fought in the sky above, earning Kent such sobriquets as Hell's Corner and Bomb Alley.

Around the coastline is a footpath, which begins at Gravesend on the south shore of the Thames Estuary, and circumvents the whole peninsula-nose via the Medway Towns, the Isle of Thanet, Dover, Folkestone and Romney Marsh, to Rye in Sussex. It is the most unlikely place for a footpath of any I know, because the question 'What purpose did or does it serve?' suggests that an answer would be neither logical nor convincing. But the footpath has a name – the Saxon Shore Way which originally connected a series of forts built by the Romans to keep Saxon marauders at bay. Since that time many other historic sites have grown up along its route, and that the Saxons subsequently used what had been designed against them is hardly open to doubt. One could just as much call it the Coastguard Path, for one imagines, having seen its creeks and indent-ations, that brandy and illegal immigrants, as well as refugees, have also crossed it on their way in. Every front door has a back door, and as often as not they are quite close together. Occasionally they are one and the same.

The coastline offers the pleasure of a long tramp of 140 miles, and can claim to be one of the most variable long-distance walks in Britain. It is a coastal, rural, industrial, urban and, above all, a historical walk. Each definition can be broken down still further because, as already stated, the military aspect, to judge by the number of forts and castles, often predominates.

The only thing to do, after arrangements for free days are made, is to set off. If one is a hog for sore feet one can do the whole lot at a gulp, taking nine days, for the walk has been conveniently divided by the Kent Rights of Way Council into stages varying from 12 to 22 miles. These I shall keep to, but before beginning there are maps to acquire, boots to fit, and a light rucksack to put on the back.

I carried the Kent Rights of Way Council booklet *The Saxon Shore Way*, which is essential, as it gives generally adequate directions, and strip-map diagrams with which to follow them. But having always been a good customer of the Ordnance Survey, I bought sheets of the 1:25,000 maps to cover the whole route. All maps are worth the price, providing you can afford them, for they will always be usable again, and there is no better way of recalling each hamlet, wood, hill, jetty and tidal indentation from the armchair, or while your feet are in a bowl of salt water and you wonder what madness induced you to undertake such futile trekking.

An essential item, of little weight, was a copy of the Estate Publications' *Atlas of Town Plans of Kent*, which contains street maps of eighteen built-up areas passed through during the course of the walk. Coming from open country where map reading is comparatively easy, and walking into the confined layout of a town, it is comforting to have these clear plans with well-labelled streets to guide the way through.

Another useful object in my kit was a prismatic compass, which I had occasion to sight enough times to justify its weight, as well as a constantly used pair of binoculars. Otherwise, there was a large tea flask, which weighs less and less as the day wears on, and enough food for lunch, plus a change of socks, shirt and underwear, a pair of light shoes for evening at hotel or bed-and-breakfast place, a sweater, a clasp knife, a notebook and the *Penguin Guide to Kent* for 1955.

Since I was not backpacking, the rucksack weighed only fourteen pounds and was never an encumbrance. For a walker, as with a poet, feet are most important. When the feet lose their easy rhythm – by blisters, callouses or swellings – the expedition comes to a halt. One can always slog on if an enemy is behind, or if a sweetheart is waiting somewhere in front, but a pleasurable ramble is out of the question when the feet seriously baulk. If they do, one is never far, on this walk, from railway station or bus – which has much to be said for it. It is not the retreat from Mons (or Moscow) or the advance to relieve Lucknow (or Mafeking), and whenever I felt it becoming so, I stopped for a day or two and then, with energy regained, came back like a glutton for more.

Finally, this is not a guidebook. W. H. Hudson was of the opinion that such things were best left behind, and not consulted until the places had been explored, though he realized their value by saying that 'there are no really bad guidebooks, and those that are good in the highest sense are beyond praise.' I carried one in case I missed something along the way. But a guidebook is optional rather than essential.

Any competent man or woman, or half-grown child, should be able, with the help of map and compass, to find a way over stile or to the left of farmhouse. Maps, if intelligently handled, will eliminate most problems; otherwise the humanely directed, or the more patient, rambler will find word-of-mouth inquiry rewarding in a way maps can never be – providing there happens to be another pedestrian within miles.

But as there is no such thing as a perfect map or an infallible navigator, the two methods of getting economically forward are one of the most satisfying combinations it is possible to devise, with the factors of fresh air, weight, progress and slowly changing scenery on this most intriguing of footpaths to lure you along. All one needs is a rainbow's end in the distance; but you can't have everything.

Chapter Two
Thames to Medway

The day begins at Charing Cross, and on the train to Gravesend where, artfully considering that worst must come first, I intend to begin. In any case, it's clockwise, and better luck to go such a way, in order to end in Rye with at least a wry smile. You start with the worst, so that what may be the best will be paradise by the time you get there.

Clouds from the train window are seen like a Victorian steel engraving, with sun shafts breaking through. The civilized London sprawl goes on for ever, each railway cutting alive with flowers, so that I think that when the Bomb goes off (though I hope it never will) the last colour will be in such places.

Clean gasometers lift up and give way to a multistorey car park in construction. Flower gardens spread, and artificial lakes glint among groves of trees. To the right are chalk clifflets covered in plants, and houses two to a block with no parking problems, and low hills beyond. Along a riverine flatness to the left pylons lead to the Thames and across to Tilbury. Thin cranes are angled up, and there are fuel tanks by the score, while chimneys and more pylons mark the landscape.

The train runs to time and by ten o'clock I'm on the platform at Gravesend station to pick up my rucksack and make a way through streets to the river front, which is 26 miles from London Bridge by water. Ships coming into the Thames take on a pilot here, and at one time the main interest of the town was to watch the flow of shipping. It is an industrial locality, but was mentioned in the Domesday survey, and in 1401 Henry IV granted its inhabitants the sole right of carrying passengers to London Town. Those who landed at Dover often went up river by barge from Gravesend, thus appreciably shortening their footslog. The place was burned to the ground by the French in 1377 – as was Rye, the end point of this Saxon Shore Way, several times burned and sacked in the fourteenth and fifteenth centuries. Thus the pedestrian goes from one historical bonfire to another.

Gravesend has many old and interesting buildings, but I only want to get onto the Saxon Shore Way and begin the walk proper. 'At low tide, the shores present no very cheerful aspect; and the riverside features of the town are quaint rather than elegant.' Black's *Guide* goes on to say that 'To lovers of the nautical world there will be something delightful even in the flavour of the Gravesend mud. . . .'

I pass the café by the public gardens, noting that the tide is out, and the river swift, with a two-masted barque moored off the mud and caught by the slight breeze. The path leads through a long alleyway of factories and warehouses, with some activity in them. Other buildings are corrugated up, a sad though common sight of modern England. There are boatyards beyond a lock of the Thames–Medway canal to the right. The canal, opened in 1814 as far as Rochester, is now disused and goes only as far as Higham – according to the map.

Some marine industrial work is still going on. The smell of prime planks comes from acres of woodyards, strongly reminiscent. There are cranes on the riverbank, and loud hammering sounds from invisible breakers and sorters in a scrapyard. The river is half a mile wide, and from Tilbury on the northern bank Queen Elizabeth mustered her troops to meet the Spanish Armada in 1588. Luckily, like the French under Napoleon, and the Germans of Hitler's time, they never landed; otherwise they might have had the same success as the Normans in 1066 – and then where would the English have been?

The Ship and Lobster pub is the last refreshment point for many a mile and, being passed at half past ten in the morning, could not be used. Licensing hours erode the hiker's faith in the flexibility of the commercial system. Country pubs should keep an open door for the benefit of the passing wayfarer from April to October. Chagrin is born out of such thirst, but there is nothing to do but pass on, pub doors appearing notoriously heavy, even to hiker's boots.

The track is a concrete walk, and the four-foot-high wall to the left is not high enough to block views over the river. The Port of London Sanitary Hospital, now disused, lies in gloomy acres of brambles and nettles. The sick and the scurvy were brought here from ships passing Gravesend, many having gained their last view of the green homeland only to die before they could enjoy further success, so that Gravesend became the grave's beginning.

The real footpath starts beyond the hospital, soil dry underfoot. Teasel, agrimony, Queen Anne's lace and dandelion add colour. Gulls reconnoitre the river mud, and a yellow-funnelled freighter called *Bexley* is coming smartly up river. The coastguard station, to which I suppose all ships report, has a direction-finding loop and a radar scanner on the roof. From their lookout they have a perfect view of the raised footpath during the day, so that whoever leaves Gravesend or goes towards it is fully visible.

No flags fly from the silent rifle range. The long arm of a gravel transporter goes almost to mid-river, and on its massive supports closer to the bank someone has risked his (or maybe her) life to add to the graffiti by painting the name ANDY FUNK, and for ten minutes I wonder who he was, what kind of a career he now pursues, and whether one day his name won't dazzle from a more metropolitan stand than this. Maybe he is already famous, and I don't know it.

Small boats lie on the mud. An enormous power station stands on the flat northern shore which is all pylons, aerials, chimneys and cranes, and a few low trees. The four chimneys of the power station follow me for miles. Morning-glories along the path have some of their white trumpets closed, but an equal number are open, as if they can't come to a consensus as to whether or not it will rain. Cabbage whites and tortoiseshell butterflies drift up, and settle back on the path when I have gone by.

A peep of sun comes from the ragged clouds, and visibility is 3 miles. The footpath is well marked, the river an indisputable guide, dried mud and small grey stones underfoot. I am followed by the noise of invisible trains and steam hammers. How many miles before all noise is left behind? There is driftwood on the strand, as well as eggboxes, a blue plastic milk crate and indestructible plastic bags. River-mud smells, and the tang of the sea, as well as an odour from grass and vegetation inland, allowing my senses to sort out the various strata of reminiscence. This walk is to be distinguished by its smells.

Hills are in view 6 miles farther on; but the Thames still holds most interest. A tug called *Sun Essex* is moored, and a dredger named *Cambourne*, with a green funnel, an immaculate white bridge structure aft, and many red-ochred cranes along the decks, passes by.

Two men are loading planks of driftwood onto a modified pram trolley. One or two others are fishing. Boys are digging in the mud, peering as if to find treasure, or something edible.

Murray's *Handbook for Kent*, 1877, says of this area: 'North of Higham stretches away a dreary ague-haunted district, formed by the tongue of low chalk land, surrounded by a broad hem of marsh, lying between the Thames and the Medway.' But I also remember how in *The Way of All Flesh* Ernest Pontifex, recalling his childhood Sunday walks here, considered the area salubrious enough to let his own children be brought up by 'a couple who lived on the waterside a few miles below Gravesend, just where the sea was beginning'. Samuel Butler writes: 'I did not see how children could live in a better physical atmosphere than this, and applauded the selection which Ernest had made on behalf of his youngsters.'

The footpath is like a road in the desert, a couple of hundred yards wide, and marked by all kinds of vehicles. The surface is of dried mud and grass clumps, baked and split as if it had recently been under water and then dried by the sun.

Shornemead Fort, surrounded by trees, looks like an oasis. It is my first positive landmark, a squat solid construction, in ruins not from bombardment but due to age and deliberate demolition. Clambering over huge pieces of masonry, I let myself down into the interior court. Piranesi would have sketched it well. I note the dozen or so immense embrasures which command the river. Now they are gunless, many obstructed by bushes. Rusting iron, from which the guns have been wrenched, and still fixed into the concrete, is twisted like so many pieces of fuse wire. The fort was once armed with the heaviest ordnance, and furnished with torpedoes.

Colonel George Hanger, in *Reflections on the Menaced Invasion* (1804) recommended that 'Another battery should also be made about midway on the Kent side, between the above work [Tilbury] and the end of the marshes above Higham. . . . These works will effectually prevent the enemy's shipping from laying in the Hope . . .', and 'only two thirty-two pounders, at a proper distance, will drive the largest ship in the navy from her moorings, and more especially if there is a supply of red-hot shot'. The colonel had spent four years partridge shooting over this part of Kent, and knew it well.

The last shots fired by guns on the other side of the river at Tilbury were aimed at British warships during the Mutiny of the Nore in 1797, when sailors finally protested against the scandalous conditions of that time. With some exceptions they were treated worse than the slaves that the rest of the population were supposed not to be, due to the sloth, idleness, incompetence and sadism of their officers.

Under the influence of their elected delegates, few excesses were committed by the sailors during the mutiny. Many of those delegates were hanged afterwards for their trouble. In many instances, being better educated and more articulate, they were forced by the sailors into their positions of responsibility. The demands were modest and just, and the lower deck remained loyal to the King and the Board of Admiralty. The moderation they showed was perhaps their undoing: they had the strength to take London or, by going over to the French, to defeat England absolutely. The mutiny collapsed, and the flogging, hanging and imprisonment commenced – though conditions did improve slightly. Seven of the mutinous ships were to fight tenaciously at the Battle of Camperdown shortly afterwards.

A few miles out of Gravesend, a salmon-coloured, unmanned lighthouse emits a melancholy hoot three times a minute, the noise as if a huge seabird is caught in a trap and, though pleading with appalling

Shornemead Fort

regularity for assistance, has little hope of relief. The mournful bleat follows for miles. A lone fisherman at his rods keeps a bicycle close by. The elevated path narrows, and turns north to the jetty at Cliffe Fort.

A seventy-foot hulk lies in the mud, plank-bones stripped clean by time and water, all superstructure gone, hollowed out and holed. There is a small boat marina behind the fort, and *The Eastgate* of Grimsby is at the jetty, taking on oil, to judge by the placarded exhortations not to smoke.

Cliffe Fort is another place recommended by Colonel Hanger for fortification. Realizing the unhealthiness of the shore, he suggested leaving only a small guard in the redoubt, and allowing the men to camp on high ground near Cliffe village, half an hour's march away. It was thought that Napoleon might begin his invasion of England here.

On Monday, 14 May 1877, the barge *Magog* landed a gun at the jetty, onto a railway waggon which immediately subsided and deposited the

Cliffe Fort

Above and opposite
Cliffe lagoon

gun into the mud. Eight days later a captain and forty men came from Sheerness to assist in getting it out and into the fort. By now the piece was three feet from the remains of the tramway, and two feet under the mud.

The gun was sinking fast, but a tricky bit of engineering was evolved to try to raise it. This included strengthening the sea wall, building a dam so that no more water would come in and increase the viscosity of the mud, erecting platforms to prevent it from sinking farther, and instituting a system of pulleys. Forty-six men working full time for ten days finally lifted it clear and got it into the fort. Where it is now is hard to guess. The life of a gun was short, with new models ever coming out of Woolwich Arsenal.

The sun comes out. A bank of shingle blocks the footpath, yet the way is obvious and I climb over with clashing boots. It is a coastline of shooting butts, crumbling jetties and rotting boats, the detritus of endeavour, the decline of industry, the laying down of obsolescent defences, reminding me of the Erewash valley and parts of Shropshire.

The humming noise of industry is still mysteriously alive in its own ruins, perhaps ever renewing itself, sounds dominated however by birds wheeling and whistling in the slight breeze. Huge harvests of blackberries will soon be ready; brambles near the closed-off fort grow like hillocks, all covered with hard early fruit.

In spite of excellent maps and firm directions in the booklet guide, I diverge from the route and in retracing my steps go along a new road in the making. Enormous lorries pass to and fro, and a sidewalk is impossible because the grass is too long to make it easy. So I use the road, which seems to be paved with soot, hardened by traffic driving along the middle at great speed. By the edge of the road, where it is safest to walk, the soot has become pure dust.

A short cut takes me through an amphitheatre of burned-out motorcars, and having regained the lane which runs along a causeway through a series of lagoons, I sit on a piece of abandoned agricultural machinery and eat lunch.

The east-southeasterly track is motorable, and the owners of a few parked cars fish slyly between almost concealing bushes. A fuel-tank depot lies in my general direction, and the green jut of Allen's Hill rises eighty feet in front. The lagoons to either side of the track are split into rectangular ponds by slender causeways of land, a sort of placid Dead Sea cut off from its main source of ocean, specially compartmented for the sun

to heat. Hard to know how the divisions came to be there, unless they were a barge dock at some time. The nearest topographical equivalent is of a fish farm in Israel.

The hut of the 'Well Come Fishing Club' is in ruins. By the petrol depot the path becomes a maze among bushes at the foot of chalk cliffs, but I make my way left, take the wrong fork from the road and ascend Allen's Hill by a cornfield. A radar scanner on a tower keeps its eternal turning lookout for all that passes along the Thames, foolproof technology ensuring that no foreigner either of flesh or boatwood coming ashore will have even a sporting chance.

The lane into Cliffe village turns into a street of houses with such Australian names as Kangaroo Villas (1904), and individual dwellings labelled Victoria, Australia, Swan Hill and Murray Downs, all four attached in mutual antipodean compatibility and comfort.

The Six Bells was a cool pub with all doors open. So I put back a pint of shandy, glad at finding the place where it should have been on such a day.

During the seventh and two following centuries numerous councils of the Saxon Church were held at Cliffe. Beacons were erected here in the time of Richard II to warn of the approach of any hostile vessels, and in 1804 a sharp watch was maintained for the advent of Bonaparte.

It seems a sleepy place as I make my way by Amy Terrace (1890) and Holmesdale Cottages (1894). Much building went on in the twenty years before the First World War. Perhaps officers and masters of sailing ships retired here, to walk the heights with telescopes and see familiar ships go by.

On the well-marked path a woman and two children, and a nondescript black dog, walk fifty yards in front. Potatoes are planted to the left. Corn to the right is flat, in wave on yellow wave, while some way in front smoke rises in a line as if from a battlefield, a layer of flame here and there at the edges of the field like small hungry animals that will leave nothing uneaten. The line of flame, yellow in front and black behind, misses nought in its clean sweep of stubble. But it is a fire without substance, having only straw and chaff on which to grip, and so it becomes easily extinct by fences or the edge of a lane.

It is good to be in countryside, with real horizons all around. There is nine-tenths cloud, but its ceiling is quite high which, though keeping the sun out, seems certain to hold the heat in. A huge oil tanker going down river is viewed out of one eye, while the other sees a young gangly adolescent hare with big ears running across the black stubble towards a lush meadow on the other side of the track. A mare and foal under a tree pay no attention as it leaps by.

On Cooling Lane a rabbit has been pounded flat by traffic. The gothic ruin of the castle has black pillars growing from collars of vegetation, a perfect eight-acre stand-in for the Castle of Otranto. Bats must fly about on the night of the full moon, and owls quietly fulminate during its absence. In contrast, the fifteenth-century gateway, with towers forty feet high and impressively machicolated, indicates the glorious state of the castle in better days.

John de Cobham fortified the manor house in 1380 because the coastal towns and villages, including Gravesend, had just been burnt and pillaged by Frenchmen and Spaniards. However, the only shots fired in anger were during periods of civil disturbance, in which times the square castle was moated. Cooling village had been in the hands of the Cobhams since the reign of Edward I. Sir John Oldcastle, the supposed original of Falstaff, inherited it by marriage and assumed the title of Lord Cobham. He was the leader of the Lollards, and shut himself up here when accused of heresy by Archbishop Arundel. But he was finally arrested and, after escaping from the Tower of London, was recaptured, tried and executed in 1417.

When Sir Thomas Wyatt attacked the place in 1554, in the cause of Protestantism (during the first year of Bloody Mary's reign, to whose

Cooling

Cooling Castle

Opposite Cooling churchyard: graves as Dickens describes those of Pip's brothers and sisters

Spanish marriage he objected), he failed to capture it, in spite of six pieces of artillery which did considerable damage. The Lord Cobham of the day defended it so skilfully that the siege had to be raised, and Wyatt marched on to Gravesend. The insurrection was not sufficiently supported to be successful. He was driven from Southwark by Sir John Bridges, who threatened to open fire with the guns from the Tower of London. After various manoeuvres Wyatt surrendered. He had no defence at the trial, though his life might have been spared had he confessed sufficiently to implicate Mary's sister, the future Queen Elizabeth, and thus cause her execution. This he refused to do, and saved England from Roman Catholic domination.

Just inside the gate is a modern-looking house, incongruous because it is as suburbanly peaceful as the castle is grim. The footpath goes behind the houses and the church and comes conveniently out on the road again at the Horseshoe and Castle which, about to close for the afternoon, just has time to supply me with the last pint for many a long hour.

The lane is called Pip's View, because Cooling Marshes to the north figure in the opening pages of *Great Expectations*, Pip's encounter with Magwitch, the escaped convict, taking place in Cooling churchyard. I have a pastel portrait of Magwitch, as acted by Bransby Williams at the Nottingham Theatre Royal in 1947, done by my Uncle Frederick, and the thin hard lines of the hunted man are exactly delineated.

The track turns north after Child's Farm, and then northeast to Bromhey Farm, in whose vast barns onions are being sorted and packed. One small discarded piece has rolled out, so I pick it up to eat later with my bread and cheese – though it was the strongest onion I'd ever tasted. In fact, mounds of unsuitable onions lay across from the machinery, ready to be swept away.

Pear trees prosper to the left, while apples flourish to the right, rows like ranks of soldiers, all with white gaiters neatly fastened to the lower trunks. On the dusty track by Eastborough Farm I pick up a couple of apples, munching as I go towards the mast of a disused radio station. From this point I am supposed to turn right and ascend to a gate leading into High Halstow nature reserve.

There are no track markings, and after a false turn through a field and beyond the edge of a wood, I come back to the lane and find the right place. Across the marshes a ship floats, huge and serene, as if on its way along the milky sky. There is no visible track, so I measure the angle on the map and go uphill on a compass bearing, through orchards and a barley field in a straight line towards the wooded summit, which brings me exactly to the gate and into the coolness of the nature reserve.

Along the shady path people edge silently by, staring into vegetation as they watch your progress. One couple push a pram, out on a stroll from High Halstow. The Royal Society for the Protection of Birds maintains a heronry here, but no herons are to be seen, though it is one of the largest in Europe. The nesting areas are far from the path, and special permission is needed to see them.

I again miss the correct footpath. Either they are not evident on the ground, or there are so many more than are indicated on the map. This is often the case around a village, where to find the right path needs half an hour's surveying work. I skirt the new houses, and walk along the road via Jackson's Corner. From the A228 I go into several acres of broken cars and impenetrable brambles behind a filling station to find the footpath again. Not deterred by such a wilderness, I clamber, zigzag, and batter through a hedge, and finally get back on course, with the feeling that some property owners deliberately try to obstruct rights of way. Walkers in Saxon days wouldn't worry about keeping to mathematically placed lines, but would go where the mood took them, as long as the general direction was maintained.

From now on the route is southerly. Ropers Farm is abandoned, tin roof banging in the wind. The Medway comes into view, milky water and *Opposite* Cockham Fort

a wide sweep of shore. A huge power station at Kingsnorth has enormous chimneys to beam on. A dredger is latched to a pier, and there is land in the distance.

The path is unmistakable, a cart track through corn, uncut on one side and burnt on the other. Across the Hoo road is a solid old-fashioned school (1875) of the kind I attended as a child, no doubt the same sort my mother went to as well, red-bricked and harmonious in design, surrounded by a low wall.

On the lane to Abbot's Court Farm is an ivy-and-bramble-covered machine-gun post, its field of fire long since forgotten. At the Medway there is a smell of mud, seawater and new-mown hay, soon replaced by the reek of smoke and flame. The sea-wall path runs by fields on which stubble has been lit, and the wind blows obliquely from the direction I'll soon be walking in. The flame is separated from the track by a ditch and a hedge, and I can avoid it only by going into the water. The line of hedge for a hundred yards erupts into flame, which is blown towards the sea. Even to turn back is difficult, and I run the distance holding my breath so as not to be asphyxiated by smoke or singed in the flames. The noise, like that of a stream of rushing water, follows for a long time after I get clear.

The path through a caravan park enables me to see onto the porches and into the windows of mobile homes, where people are watching television or sitting down to evening drinks.

By boatyards and breakwaters, workshops, marinas and yacht clubs, the winding and endless way goes on. Sometimes it is only possible to go along the stony strand itself, which is painful to the feet. Woods rise steeply up the hill to my right, and the foliage is too thick to find a path through, though I make an occasional attempt, only to be funnelled back to the beach.

A concrete blockhouse, built on gravel and shingle, its foundations washed loose by the tide, lies at a crazy angle, apertures fit only for firing into the sky, a relic of the Second World War still waiting for the promised invasion.

Two views of Cockham Wood

Chatham dockyard, opposite the village of Upnor, is soon to become redundant in the dismantling of Britain's industrial base – easy to kill and never to be recovered. Skill will go under the hammer of demolition. What remains of goodwill is to be scattered. There seems something gleeful about the squandering of so many good trades.

Upnor is a Medway boating village with a steep street of charming houses going down to the water. It will no doubt look on at the dismantling of Chatham dockyard, as did its fort which, erected in 1561, failed to prevent the Dutch raid under Admiral de Ruyter in 1667. Upnor Castle watched the destruction of several English ships, one being the *Royal Oak* of 80 guns, whose commander, Captain Douglas, defended his vessel with great valour, observing, when it was deemed expedient for him to take to the boats, that a Douglas was never known to quit his post without orders – and so went down with his ship. Upnor Castle is now a military storehouse.

Two views of Upnor Castle

The public houses are open again, so a twenty-minute break for the slaking of thirst takes place. Are the last few miles of any day's walk always so dreary? If I had passed here first thing in the morning the miles might not have seemed so long. The last stretch from Upnor is all squalor and decay, litter scattered on gravel and stunted bushes.

In a creek, by the site of a former convict garden, a black wooden barge is stuck in the muddy inlet, a line of drying clothes attached from it to a pole on shore. Nearby a motorbike is half covered with oil cloth, and not far away in the marshy mire is a decrepit open two-seater touring car, as if the occupants had driven it there and, realizing that it would be more serious than a lark to get it out, had left it and gone on their merry way to Rochester.

The barge is snug in the mud, stove-pipe chimney emitting smoke for tea or supper, well away from the town, an almost perfect habitation in these overpopulated days. A big black dog scratches itself, and stares at me.

Two paths along brick tracks run parallel, and I choose the wrong one, ending at the top of a slope faced by a tall wire fence. Rather than go back I sling my rucksack over, then wonder how I am going to follow. After a few minutes a drop of rain comes down, so I take a running jump and, without knowing how it was done, am on the other side.

Through gas dumps and coal depots the path winds, and descends to the station at Strood, the end of the first day's walk. A pub provides my final pint, but I've drunk so much shandy that the aftertaste is one of soap.

The problem is to find a bed and, as the streets look unpromising, I decide to try Rochester. Having walked 20 miles from the Thames to the Medway, a bit more will make no difference. Crossing the bridge at half past seven, the ironwork gives only tantalizing glimpses of the view, and the steel-engraving half-copper twilight for which the Medway at Rochester is famous.

There is little traffic where Watling Street spans the only real water barrier on its way to London. Old guidebooks list the numbers of royalty who have crossed here – either coming or going – and mention is made in one of how 'the good and gentle Victoria several times passed through Rochester's streets on her way to the military hospital at Chatham, where it has been her noble pleasure to soothe and encourage her wounded Crimean heroes'.

The tourist office on the High Street shows a list of hotels, guest houses and bed-and-breakfast establishments in its window, but only phone numbers are given, and I am too tired to find out where a likely one might be and go there. My feet ache after more than 20 miles. So did David Copperfield's on his hike to Canterbury, or Tess D'Urberville's on her wanderings across Dorset. I pass the three hotels on the High Street and, deciding on the Gordon, go in to discover that they have a single room.

Sitting in the empty bar, I eat a supper of sandwiches and drink two huge pots of tea in an attempt to rehydrate myself after sweating so much on the march. The concatenating yacker of a television set comes from the lounge down the steps next door.

Chapter Three
Medway to the Swale

No one likes being followed, least of all a walker, but throughout the day, almost until the Swale comes into view, the heaped-up black stack of Kingsnorth power station is always there whenever I turn to see how far I have come, or to get a backward glance at the scenery which I have only seen clearly from the front. The chimney seems to be malevolently following, because the distance never appears to increase between us. I don't resent the shape or purpose of the power station but only, to a certain degree, the intimidating landmark of navigation. There is no other for miles around. In the Middle Ages a footslogger beamed himself on the spire of the next cathedral city. Today he selects a convenient power station and homes in on that.

Sanctuary from the power station is effective in the shelter of Rochester High Street, as is that offered by the cathedral, in which I spend half an hour observing the stately architecture and reading the various memorial stones to soldiers and sailors who died young. I remember Ellis Smith, an ex-Royal Marine who lived next door, and had done twelve years with the colours, till he was pensioned off as sick. Wheezing and gasping, he used to tell how, in the fighting against the Bolsheviks in north Russia, he would drive a horse and cart to collect corpses after the skirmishing. He also talked of his carefree times in Chatham, and died at about forty years of age, robust but deadly pale.

This is a walkbook rather than a guidebook, so others must tell of the treasures of Rochester. According to Penguin, Baedeker, Blue Guide and Murray, there are plenty. But I want to get on, though I spend some time in secondhand bookshops along the High Street. I also buy a packet of plasters from a chemist's, where a cheerful and obliging girl cuts them neatly into the required sizes.

Hebrew lettering across the road decorates a romanesque-style

Naval memorial, Rochester, and (*below*) the Nautical Bookshop

Rochester Castle and Cathedral

synagogue built in 1869. The Saxon Shore Way, still in the streets of the Medway Towns, leads up to open ground known as the Great Lines, two hundred feet above sea level. In latter days field operations, imitation battles and grand reviews took place here. One remembers the situation of Mr Pickwick, when he was exposed to the fury of blank cartridges and the rush of a charging regiment.

The space is famous today for a naval war memorial, the tall obelisk designed by Sir Robert Lorimer in 1924. After the Second World War Sir Edward Maufe added quadrant walls. The inside structure has the names of 35,000 naval personnel who died during the Great War, and the interior denotes those who perished in the second. There is no separate section for the Fleet Air Arm, for which force I volunteered at the age of seventeen.

Dickens in Rochester: his
chalet, where he wrote many of
his novels was rebuilt in
Rochester next to the Dickens
Centre, and scenes at the
Rochester Dickens Festival

The memorial matches the sombre and equally huge erection of the Menin Gate at Ypres in Belgium, which records the deaths of 70,000 men who died in the salient and have no known graves. Identical memorials to this naval construction have been built at Plymouth and Southsea. The massive concrete figures of sailors seem indifferent to either life or death, and certainly to the rain which begins as I close the gate and go back onto the common.

A few scraggy ponies graze, and getting back to the houses, I follow the road through Gillingham, a total of more than 5 miles before the Medway streets are done with. Normal life goes on, Saxon ghosts unseen or ignored. The Strand is a park and fairground, and I shelter in the café from occasional flurries of chill rain and a bracing north wind. When raindrops hit a map, it's like slumwater striking the surface of an old master painting.

There were at least fifty listed buildings in the naval base at Chatham

Opposite The ropery, nearly a quarter of a mile long, one of the longest buildings in the country

Above The alleyway between the ropery and the old chain compound

The Strand, Gillingham

Back in tidal waters, by marsh, creek and reach, the smell of estuary mud assails, a reassuring tang of progress. Odours of the fishy sea are more stimulating to the lungs than the reek of motor traffic. The tide is out, and clumps of greenery speckle the dark ooze. Small craft stay snugly at anchor.

The squalor that comes and goes is rather the graveyard of activity and endeavour: wrecked boats, rubbish dumps, old cars, shutdown workshops; yet there are also occupied slipways, and workplaces where people bang with hammers and move knowingly about. The rain has stopped, but the path is muddy. Mud underfoot pads the boots and splatters trousers. For the walker, as for the soldier in the First World War, the enemy is mud. The elevated path winds in and out of small bays and inlets.

A boy stands before me, looking at his smart racing bike: 'Can you tell me the time, please?' His hair is well cut. He is about thirteen, and wears a windcheater.

'Twelve o'clock,' I say, having drawn out my watch.

'Have you got a penknife?' he asks.

'Penknife? What for?'

He shows his rear wheel. Solid mud is so clogged between tyre and mudguard that it isn't possible to turn. He can't even push – having ridden to a standstill. I put down my rucksack and get to work with my old black RAF-issue knife, not using the blade, as he assumes I will, since it might cut the tyre, but pulling out the spike, which I never really believed was used only for extracting stones from horses' hooves. I once used the knife in the Malayan jungle, I said, because silence seems unnatural while I work. There was plenty of mud there, I tell him, 'shooting a line', as we used to say, though it is true enough. Apart from a few maps and a cap badge, it's the only equipment I have left.

Eastcourt Meadows
Country Park

Both wheels spin free, so he thanks me and pushes the bike carefully to the nearest paved lane. Friendly people who pass never merely nod good morning but, like one elderly man who looked as if he had spent all his life on or with boats, say: 'I'll bet the day's going to be pleasant for you' – or some such encouraging remark. They carry an atmosphere of seafaring and travelling. It's in cars and before television sets that people cease to be human. In the first case they are living for machinery, and in the second the machine lives for them. When people meet on a footpath by the shore, they have got there by using either their own feet, or the wind in a sail, and no machine is present to distort the goodwill as they pass by.

Five hulks were sunk to form a breakwater, long boats filled with concrete whose wooden frames have long since gone, so that the shape of the boats remains. The tide is far out, and gulls reconnoitre mud rivers

Opposite Bloors Wharf

Near Otterham Quay

curving like miniature Amazons when seen from the raised footpath. Islands and tributaries stretch from the green water right up to the wharves. When the sea comes in such great and seemingly distinct rivers will be buried, and when the tide recedes they will reappear in different forms. Every day the map changes.

The only equipment lacking is the wherewithal to brew up, tackle without which no walker can claim independence, or go very far off the beaten track. Thirst makes me crave a spirit stove and kettle to make tea strong enough to stand a spoon in. Cafés and hotels serve tea from teabags, which produce a liquid I abominate. Are they used because they are cheap, and less trouble to dispose of? The places which do not use them should be starred with the honourable sign of a golden cup and saucer in

Near Gillingham

Opposite Near Gillingham, with Kingsnorth power station in the background

the guidebooks. On asking for tea at establishments along the road, one ought to be given the choice of tealeaf tea or teabag liquid, even though the price might be higher. The so-called best hotels use teabags, and the only one I stayed at recently that didn't was the Maid's Head in Norwich.

As a child I remember an unemployed man walking along the backyards calling out: 'Can anyone spare a cup o' tea for a bloke on tramp?' and though not much was available, the mug of tea forthcoming was certainly genuine enough. Today he would get teabag wash, because the English make tea as the Spanish did thirty years ago. But the Spaniards had some excuse, and they at least served good coffee. Teabag

tea, while indisputably wet and warm (and sweet if you like white sugar), is unfit to drink as far as the quality is concerned.

The time of the day seems important to boys, because a group comes up from the shoreline at one o'clock to ask. I suppose they have been told to get home for lunch at a certain hour. The sky is clearing. Vapour trails at 18,000 feet are a long line going from nowhere to nowhere, like the rest of us, I suppose, beginning in the blue and ending in the black. Inland are apple orchards, fruit regions contrasting now with the shore line. I pass Horrid Hill and Sharp's Green, with the sewage works of Motney peninsula odoriferous in the distance.

The walk directs me around Motney Hill, but I cut the corner as no doubt the Romans or the Saxons did. Crude National Front signs are seen twice, demented daubings occasionally found in such decaying areas. Maybe the Saxons carved anti-Norman slogans on the trees when the Conqueror and his followers showed no sign of going home.

The public house at Bloors Place is convenient for a lunchtime shandy, and I sit close to the door so as not to foul the landlord's fine carpet with mudcaked boots. Half a mile along a minor road, facing the traffic flow, brings me to another orchard footpath to Otterham Quay. It trundles a mere few hundred yards, then comes to a factory area and more road, then a delightful path through extensive plum and apple plantations, well fenced on either side to keep out the thirsty light-fingered wayfarer.

Halfway along I sit down to lunch of rye bread and Polish sausage, enjoying the good-weather rest, being now 8 miles along in my day's quota. One meets fewer people on a purely rural walk than on those

Opposite Upchurch

Factory area near Rainham

promenades by the sea, or on riverbanks. The trees of the orchards stand in ranks, emphasizing the isolation, taking my eyes from the clouds as I plod on to the next navigational point – in this case bungalows on the outskirts of Upchurch, from where the track resumes in a northerly direction.

Looking for the footpath to Ham Green, I reconnoitre the road at Wetham Green but cannot find a plain way in. Going through a hedge, I am in someone's back garden, the evidence for which is a child's swing, a picnic table, a rubber swimming pool, and a dog kennel which for the moment looks abandoned. A five-year-old girl stares from a rocking horse. The bulge at the seat of her jeans suggests that she has not yet reached the age of continence. A dummy hangs from her neck by a length of post-office string. She's going to cry, so I smile and wave. She is strong, pulls at the head of the horse, and bangs its chin on the patio tiles. Animals ought to be thankful that toys were invented. She looks at me, and does it again. I make a sign that she ought to leave the poor beast alone, wooden though it is. She grasps the horse's hair, as if to pull the head off altogether, then changes her mind, looks at me for a few seconds, and begins to scream.

I hear furniture falling and doors banging from inside the house, as well as a shriek of irritation which suggests no one believes in her distress – or at least if they do they can't be bothered to come out and do anything about it. I backtrack to the road, and look for another path. The one I find seems public enough, goes through a cornfield where a man and a woman are loading hay onto a dray. Their savage dog comes furiously barking towards me, and though there is a fence bordering the path, I suppose the hound won't need much ingenuity to get over and at me. A harsh word or two never comes amiss with a dog, and in order to deter it I call out: 'If you take a bite out of my ankle, it'll cost you a bob or two!'

At which the woman calls angrily: 'What did you say?'

I reply with equal firmness that I was merely passing the time of day with her dog, a response which seems to satisfy her, and also the dog, especially when the man calls it sharply to heel.

I get back to the road through a poultry farm, quacked at by geese, and then go on by Twinney Acre and Frog Farm. There are brick works, wharves, sewage works and saltings to the east. I carry out more jungle-like travelling to stay on the correct alignment. A machete would have made the going easier through a zone of tall nettles. The odd branch and bramble is thrown in for good measure between two fences, a bottleneck

Orchard, Twinney Creek

along which I must pass. I stamp the herbage down for a while, till I seem only to impact the resistance. I also feel mud and then water underfoot, as if a spring has been diverted there. I backtrack, force a way through the fence, and take myself diagonally across a couple of unobstructed fields to where two teenage girls tend their horses.

At the supermarket in Lower Halstow I buy chocolate, and a pint of cold milk which I guzzle on the spot so as to leave the bottle in a convenient crate by the door. Halstow church has a twelfth-century leaden front, discovered after the plaster round it was split by the concussion of gunfire during the First World War, though the nearest point of the front was 70 miles away.

The footpath by Stray Farm parallels the road, but is unmarked, and I hesitate until a man on a tractor points to the stile which leads back to the road. Beyond Great Barksore the Funton footpath begins, but to get on it means going through a field occupied by a bull and six cows. I always believe possession to be nine-tenths of the law, and the bull looking at me certainly knows that it possesses the field. The law says I can go through, but a bull in attendance with a pack of cows is no child with a dummy around its neck.

The eye-glitter, and thread of steam coming from the left nostril, not to mention a faint twitch of the right hoof, tell me there'll be no glamour in entering such a perilous situation – especially for the dubious benefit of a footpath of which at this stage there is no proper trace. In fact, it is not delineated at all. Even if I get by the bull without let or hindrance I'm bound to lose the footpath sooner or later.

Near Lower Halstow

Opposite Near Stray Farm

Not that I imagine myself unable to run if chased; but as I gaze at the undoubtedly handsome beast, which has already come from the middle of the field to sniff the wind of my deliberations, I am not altogether certain that any run will be fast enough. It is a common situation for ramblers, but I am afraid that what evasive tactics I can muster might prove somewhat rusty. A mistake under such circumstances is likely to be one too many. In other words, I will not take the risk, especially with a fourteen-pound hump on my back. Whether or not I miss the most scenic part of the trek seems unimportant.

Another matter is that my feet are sore, and I can't afford too much countermarching should the footpath disappear, or if I otherwise miss it at awkward places. My heels are complete blisters, separate water cushions under my feet. I am reminded of those army reservists who, recalled to the colours in 1914, went straight from their workshops and offices and set out for France. After the Battle of Mons in Belgium the Great Retreat began, during which most of them marched at least 200 miles in thirteen days. Though many discarded various parts of their equipment, an army was still in being when the retreat stopped, which was able to advance once more towards the Germans.

About halfway through the retreat one battalion, at rest in a village square, was all done up and unable to move. An officer was in despair because nothing he said or did could get them to march. Inspired perhaps by Mars himself, he went into a toyshop, bought a toy trumpet and a few penny whistles and, with a few other men beating on empty petrol tins, went tooting among the soldiers like the Pied Piper of Hamelin, playing 'The British Grenadiers' and 'Tipperary' until every exhausted man re-awoke and followed laughing behind him, the whole battalion gradually forming fours and marching away to safety. The officer's name was Tom Bridges, and he reached the rank of general, with a knighthood thrown in, by 1921.

The bull and I look at each other over the fence. He will resent and resist any move on my part into the field. Should I succeed in getting in, I would very quickly have to get out again. Such a manoeuvre will not advance me far along the chosen footpath, so with sore feet I move parallel to him and his cows and keep to the road, passing Funton brickworks till I come to the indentation of water known as Bedlams Bottom.

A mile to the north is Chetney Hill, 8 metres high and hardly rising above the surrounding land. The coastal features here have names like Deadmans Island, Slaughterhouse Point, Slayhills Marsh and Burntwick Island. Can these be a legacy of the prison hulks, floating hospital ships and quarantine vessels at one time moored in the area? Their great dull shapes seen against the setting sun from nearby high ground in the eighteenth century must have seemed dreadful. Thousands of unmarked graves pocked the low islands and shores of creeks which could only be reached by boat. A ship laden with people dying from bubonic plague would stay weeks and months out in the Medway marshes, where to get food or water was often impossible, and people died by the score from causes other than those for which they were originally quarantined. Some bid was eventually made for civilized treatment, and a lazarette planned on Chetney Hill. But it was never finished, and no trace of the foundations remains.

A sense of tragedy pervades the shore, even on a sunny day. A strong wind blows the expanse of Bedlams Bottom into steely ripples. When the Nore Mutiny collapsed in 1797, sailors from the various ships attemped to land here and make their escape before retribution began. Desperate efforts were made to evade constables and the local militia, but prisons round about were filled to overflowing. Many sailors drowned in their attempts to reach land. Three boatloads of mutineers from the *Inflexible*

Bedlams Bottom

made for Faversham, at which place a score of them captured a ship and sailed to freedom in Calais, sending the vessel back to its owners in charge of two boys!

The foul stench is probably from the petrochemical complex on the horizon, whose pale shapes look like the stacked pieces of the victor by a draughts board. But for high water, other stinks may be added. A high hedge along the road acts as a windbreak for the orchards behind, but leaves no space for a pedestrian to stand or rest.

Every county has its quota of rebels, but Kent seems to have had more than most, with the possible exception of East Anglia across the water. This stage of the walk brings Wat Tyler to mind. Said to have been a native of Kent or Essex, he served as a soldier in the French War, but was also marked down as 'a rogue and robber of Kent'. The rural labourers and lower-grade craftsmen suffered great hardship in the economic distress that followed the Black Death and the enactment of the Statute of Labourers in 1351. The discontent was brought to a head by the imposition of poll taxes in 1379 and 1381, and at the end of May riots broke out in Essex, at Brentwood. On 4 June violence occurred at Dartford, and two days later several thousand people, after storming the castle at Rochester, marched on Maidstone, where they elected Wat Tyler their leader.

The rising spread over the whole of Kent, with much looting and firing. On 10 June, Tyler's army took Canterbury, sacked the archbishop's palace and executed three 'traitors'. Next day, with more Kentish recruits pouring in, he led his followers to London, being joined at Maidstone by another celebrated rebel, John Ball, whom the people had freed from the archbishop's prison.

Reaching Blackheath, marching almost 40 miles in two days, they burnt the prisons in Southwark and pillaged the archbishop's palace at Lambeth. Another body of rebels from Essex camped at Mile End, north of the Thames.

Richard II, only fourteen years old, was at the Tower of London, but none of his ministers had taken any measures to oppose the rising. London Bridge had been lowered by Tyler's sympathizers, and the Kentish rebels crossed the Thames into the City, where they were joined by thousands of apprentices, artisans and, of course, criminals. They sacked palaces and burned down prisons. On the 14th, the King rode bravely out to talk with the rebels, meeting Wat Tyler at Mile End. During the tumultuous disputations several people were killed.

Much before his time – though none too soon for his political followers – Tyler wanted the immediate abolition of serfdom and the end to feudal services, as well as the removal of restrictions on freedom of labour and trade, plus a general amnesty for all insurgents. The revolt was widespread and the King had no choice but to grant their terms. While charters were being drawn up, Tyler and a group of his followers went to the Tower, captured Archbishop Sudbury and Sir Robert Hales, who were hiding in the chapel, and executed them on Tower Hill.

During the following day and night there was much general slaughter and plundering, the chief losers being Flemish merchants and lawyers. This was the worst mistake the mob could have made, for the people of trade and property now took steps to arm themselves and restore order. On 15 June, Richard went to Smithfield for more parleying, and Tyler shook his hand, only to make new demands which included the breaking-up of ecclesiastical estates for the benefit of the people, and social equality for every man.

Richard promised everything, as long as they left the royalty of the crown intact. Tyler said: 'We'll see about *that* as well, when the time comes.' At which so-called insolence, vociferations began on both sides, till Tyler said something so vile to the King that the Mayor of London, who was by his side, killed him with one thrust, helped by another from one of the King's squires.

Tyler's rebels drew their bows, but Richard galloped into the open: 'Sirs, will you shoot your King?'

Leaderless, they hesitated. To have acted would have catapulted the country into a civil war which may have caused as much despoliation as the Black Death itself and brought no real change in the social order.

'I will be your chief and captain,' said the King, 'and give you everything you want.' They needed to believe. One leader is as good as another. Any leader is better than no leader at all. To have no leader would have been like having the sky taken away. They didn't shoot. Tyler was the hero one minute, and the next it was undoubtedly the King.

Richard led his new followers to a meadow close by, talking and listening till Walworth came back from the City with sufficient companies of loyal citizens to intimidate and disperse the new men. The insurrection lasted longest in East Anglia under John Wraw and Geoffrey Lister. Over a hundred people were executed in Kent and Essex, including John Ball and Jack Straw, Tyler's chief lieutenant. None of Richard's promises for reform was kept.

The rebellion in 1450 under Jack Cade also drew its main support from the people of Kent, but Cade had less followers the nearer he got to London, where what reinforcement he did receive came after he had burned down the prisons at Southwark – not the most valuable addition to a rebel's power. As soon as Cade's men began to plunder, opposition built up strongly and quickly. They were ejected from London and harried back into the countryside, but not before some promises had been made and pardons drawn up. When the rising collapsed, Cade was captured, severely wounded, in Sussex, and died on his way to London, where the body was beheaded and quartered.

Nothing came of that disturbance either. The English like their revolutions, when they can stomach the idea at all, to be carried out tidily, with as little fuss as possible, and done under the auspices of the middle class. They generally, however, prefer to watch revolutions on the

Continent from their own safe dress circle where all seats are bookable and provided with little red opera glasses. And in such a way I also would prefer to mull on them, I decided – walking alone on a remote road of northern Kent and ascending the gentle slope of Raspberry Hill. A mob carries within it the seeds of its own and everyone's destruction.

Traffic is frequent. The houses of Willow Cottages, Chetney Cottages and the Iwade poultry farm are peaceful habitations overlooking the Swale which splits the Isle of Sheppey from the coast. In the distance are the prominent supports of Kingsferry Bridge connecting it to the mainland.

This is an area of sailors, rebels and smugglers. Jack Cade was one of the latter before he achieved the kind of fame that killed him young. The combination of sailor and rebel gives the English that peculiar and original scope for the development of their gifts. A man may go to sea (or cut himself off in other ways) because, a stranger unto himself, he rebels against having to meet whoever he might turn out to be should he stay on land, thus delaying the recognition until he can at least accomplish it in his own good time. An actual rebel, on the other hand, loses himself in the sea of the mob – with perilous consequences. Whoever associates himself with the mob is doomed to die in any attempt to alleviate common distress. But he does succeed in showing the non-rebels that corner of their soul which contributes to the acceptance of worldly wellbeing – frightened or illuminated as they might be by it. The wise man can learn from fear, and the hitherto dull person from illumination, but rebels of any sort are by their nature born to be unsuccessful, even in their rebellion.

There is something hard about this second day on the road. Progress drags at the spirit, and I long for the third day to begin. Near the end of the day miles are turning into leagues, though at least on this occasion it doesn't rain. From the rise I stop a while and look at the Swale bridge through binoculars, to watch a cargo ship threading the narrows. This coast is said by many old guidebooks to be unhealthy. I find it lonely, but not unbeautiful.

In much the same way as Ireland and Spain, Kent and Essex had more in common than with their neighbouring counties by land. The reason was ease of communication by sea. Small boats could make the crossing and it was no accident that rebellions which began in Kent always passed to Essex rather than into Sussex. And after they had been crushed in Kent, they lived a little longer in Essex.

Marshland near Kingsferry Bridge

In the 1830s there were agricultural riots in Kent. There was no acknowledged leader, but all rick burnings and threats of violence to those landowners and rich farmers who would not pay their labourers decent wages were signed 'Captain Swing'. Such notes also appeared in Essex, fomenting the same trouble and bearing a similar name.

The flat road leads to Swale station. There is a platform to stand on, but no other buildings – a halt in the middle of nowhere. Cars and lorries still queue to cross by the bridge now that the ship is through. I get on the train for Sittingbourne, and hope to find lodgings there.

Chapter Four
To Faversham

Pictures of landscape stay a long time in the mind, and return at will. Imprinted more definitively than faces, which need a photographic reminder to recall, landscapes remain true.

The third stage of the Saxon Shore Way starts from Swale station, otherwise known as Kingsferry Bridge, from which height I descend onto the shore of flat fields, pylons and powerlines. Meteorologically, the cloud is five-tenths cumulus, wind force 3 on the Beaufort scale, visibility 5 miles. The sea-wall footpath is a raised mound of earth. Small boats line the bank for two hundred yards, and across the water are the chalk, green-covered hills of Sheppey. Some slopes are built on.

Rhiddam Cottage seems derelict, though the attached haybarn is full. The raised footpath goes round Ridham Dock. White and pink clover is underfoot. Queen Anne's lace and thistles line the bank. Lanes, tracks, bits of old railway line and aerial ropeways give plenty to follow. What moral objection can there be if one enjoys turning on a tap or flicking a switch for light? In any case, nature all too quickly reclaims its own, and if you don't like the view (it is by no means total dereliction), you may turn your head to the placid waters of the Swale.

The raised footpath hides Ridham Dock. Boats bring Baltic wood for papermills near Sittingbourne. Small tortoiseshell butterflies dart up in front. Going down the bank and up again between bushes, a large fat woodpigeon, scared out of its wits, flaps vertically away.

The sun makes it a fine day, every flower a marvel of nature. There is no such thing as an ugly flower. Maybe they appear at their most beautiful the nearer they are to factory or dock squalor, just as the best part of a cheese is where the discriminating rats have begun to nibble. Rosebay blends with tall reedgrass, and even ragwort, plantain, thistle flower and common nettle attract by their multitude and vigour.

Kingsferry

A blue boat in full sail creams its way at four knots along the Swale. The tide is out, straits narrow between mud flats. The land track is a high sea wall with wide footpath. Navigation is difficult only when crossing agricultural land.

There is a stink of effluent. The Kemsley papermill, owned by Bowaters, is a grey colossus of towers and chimneys covering several hundred acres. A grit-paved road takes walkers close by the dominating mill. One is able to enjoy riverine landscape to the left. The Saxon Shore Way is a footpath of visual and olfactory contrasts. Rubbish dumps proliferate between me and the mill, heaps of domestic and industrial detritus. The connoisseur of tips would find much of interest on this route.

A rowing boat is mouldering in mud, and I wonder how long it has been there. Twenty? A hundred years? Who owned or rowed it, got pleasure or

Kemsley papermills from the Swale

his living from it? Perhaps he took the occasional sailor or pedestrian from the mainland to Sheppey. He's long dead, his boat half buried, the top cleaned by the tide, the bottom gripped by mud. Gulls squark, as they had followed the boat to and fro in life.

The unmistakable smell of coal smoke makes me think of steam trains. A fenced compound has a welcoming open gate. Workshops and small station are part of the Sittingbourne and Kemsley Light Railway, open as far as Milton Creek since 1906, and used for moving paper between Sittingbourne and Kemsley, and to ships at Ridham Dock.

The present length of 2 miles is leased from Bowaters and run by volunteers, some of whom are at work on the engines. There is a refreshment area, as well as swings for children, and the run to Sittingbourne effectively re-creates the sensation of old-fashioned coal-steam travel. Two of the engines were in use when the line opened. The sight of one pulling three carriages through the long grass of Church Marshes is both pretty and nostalgic.

Back on the path by the river, industry is left behind, the space in front coloured by the usual hawkweeds, burdock, marsh thistle and wild teasel. But a small gasometer is visible in the distance, and a factory chimney lurks behind trees. As long as I don't look back, peace of a sort reigns.

Sittingbourne and Kemsley Light Railway and the repair workshops, at the Light Railway Museum, Sittingbourne

Butterflies lifting at every step might suggest I am walking through an unfenced nature reserve. They flutter up as if, when a few feet away, I step on a hidden pedal beneath the grass that sets them flittering joyfully at their release. Subcreeks occasionally branch off, one being a breaker's yard of decrepit tugs and barges. On the other side opposite the sewage works a rusting paddle steamer is moored by a gasometer. A boarded-up house nearby was once a pub called the Brickmakers' Arms.

A man and boy below the bank are shooting pellets into the mud from air rifles. The sewage farm emits a strong sulphurous smell that horses in a field seem not to notice. There is something sinister about the last mile into Sittingbourne. I wouldn't have fancied walking here in the eighteenth century when press gangs were about. The map shows a Saxon burial ground, a large area of up-and-down tracks and clumps of greenery, among which half a dozen young lads are practising Saturday-afternoon rough stuff on their motorbikes.

Near the brickworks, Murston Nature Reserve

Skirting Sittingbourne and getting around the head of Milton Creek means passing the inevitable breakers' yards. Inside a hangar-like shed the blue flame of a cutting machine goes through metal. A nation of consumers means there is much breaking to be done. Reducing items to their basic scrap is a skill from which a living can be got. Very little raw material goes to waste. Old cars, vans, obsolescent machinery or outdated marine engines are stripped and sorted, and sold back to the smelters and melters.

It is an occupation that keeps people busy week in and week out. Lorries come and go. Workshops are big enough to have an office. The business requires fine judgement, and negotiation in acquiring and selling the material. At the back of the station, between the railway line and the creek, is the breakers' quarter; but Sittingbourne has other industries, as well as a vast Euro-terminal. The old market town has grown into an industrial centre, with cement and brickworks and fruit preserving.

Ancient boats are either left to rot or, happily in some cases, docked and carefully worked towards restoration. At the Dolphin Barge Museum is an old sail loft, and several fine-looking vessels in their private creek. A patrol of geese struts and cackles on guard at the entrance to the quay, and two Alsatian dogs eye everyone meaningfully. Such treasured objects as these barges are a target for vandals, and geese are the apposite creatures for alarm signals, with dogs as the hard line of defence if it comes to dispersing invaders.

Boys are toying with planks on a stagnant stream. Heading across open ground, small white, large white and meadow brown butterflies thrive on rubbish dumps, and are not put off by motor noises from warehouses and workshops. A peacock flits among ragwort. I see a small tortoiseshell near the Brickmakers' Arms where the soot-and-cinder path is wide enough for traffic. Rosebay is in carmine bloom. The area is covered with white, yellow and red flowers, and a few patches of baked-out thistles. A melancholy lapwing flies over old oyster beds near the Swale.

The rifle range is disused, and so is Elmley Ferry, an ancient crossing where the luckless James II was arrested by fishermen from Faversham in 1688 while trying to get out of the country. He finally did so from Rochester, at dead of night with one companion, going down to the river where a skiff took him to exile in France – much to the relief of William of Orange who wanted him out of the way.

A wrecked and mouldering steamer lies near the northern shore. The buildings of Kingshill Farm stand by a line of trees, against a slight rise of

Dolphin Barge Museum

land behind. It is a hot day, but a cooling breeze reaches the sea-wall path, which I walk to the swish of dry grass and the hum of insects, and the scatter of startled birds. All habitation and industry are left behind.

The haze of late August lies over Conyer Creek. Flowers proliferate, fields of common mallow, each a blue-pink beauty four feet high. There is the purple bloom of sea lavender that brightens many a muddy shore, as well as umbelliferous sea hulver, grey or pale blue if rain is promised. Boil up common fleabane and the fleas won't bite. Teasel and coltsfoot are like two solicitors nodding from a distance. I never can differentiate between hawkweeds, unless I have Edward Steps's three volumes in my rucksack.

Every creek has its workshops and boatyards, and Conyer is no exception; but they are on the other bank. The village is an attractive place, rendered more so by the prominent public house which for a long time is so near yet so far. Beer and shandies can almost be reached across the mud and water, but instead of the hundred yards it is half a kilometre around the two heads of the creek, negotiating slipway, dock and village street in the heat to get there before closing time – which is done with but few minutes to spare.

There are innumerable boats and smart new houses, and I walk through the clack of carpenters' hammers and the hum of flymowers to the white-fronted Ship Inn. After the serving of good drinks, the establishment puts the accent on charity, judging by the row of collection boxes at the bar. Conyer was a notorious haunt of smugglers, but now exudes an air of boatgoing respectability.

The way out leads through orchards, along a track well used by people, but especially their dogs – to judge by all the signs. A white jersey in good condition is spread on the ground, with a blue collar to fit a three-year-old. A handkerchief or sock, one can understand, but what had happened to make the child lose his sweater?

Elmley Ferry. The wartime minesweeper on the left was lived in until 1978

Back to the banks of the Swale, and mysterious Sheppey beyond, whose higher land is accentuated by mist. As I walk along there is fresh air and the smell of flowers, a distant warble of doves, the hum of insects, and the loud crying of seabirds.

Sewer-like stenches come from the oyster fisheries. A notice on Fowley Island says: NO LANDING. A boat moored nearby has a dark blue hull, and a wheelhouse of paler blue, the whole reflected below the water. At the end of the spit is a handsome tall-masted catamaran called (or perhaps it was the residence of) *Mrs Growltiger*, a superb marine edifice high out of the water and seemingly all set to go. No one is on deck, and hatches are battened as I examine it for several minutes with my binoculars.

There are hills beyond the marshes. I mull on the different classifications of peripatetic locomotion. Words like *walk, march, trudge* pass in procession for consideration. An easy rhythm is the carriage to achieve, without hurry and with no goal in mind. To exist for the moment, minus past and future, is the ideal, which comes and goes in flashes of marvellous reality.

The smell of the sea is too familiar to be unpleasant. A small aeroplane growls in the blue. White clouds to the south look placid. A skylark hovers in the milky northern sky. Disputatious gulls dot the grey surface of the water. Walking is a pleasure, but some part of the feet is always sore.

Coming to Uplees Marshes, I wondered what songs the Gunpowder Girls sang while at work. I have known from an early age what Faversham was famous for. In school at eleven, a young teacher came who, on his first day, announced that he was born in a place called Faversham. 'And do any of you', he asked, 'know where that is?'

I had recently acquired a copy of Bartholomew's *Motoring Atlas of Great Britain*, and studying every page with close attention enabled me to tell him that Faversham was in Kent – having concentrated on that county because an aunt lived there.

This seemed to surprise him, but he asked further if anyone knew what Faversham was famous for. I put up my hand: 'Gunpowder mills, sir.'

In answer as to how I knew, I stammered something about looking at maps. A short time later he left to go into the army – unless our rowdy behaviour had driven him away. I felt that my answers had been a triumph of sorts, and so Faversham has always been in my memory, especially the powder mills whose remains, forty years later, I was about to see.

Faversham has some claim to being the birthplace of gunpowder making in Britain, the first manufactory established in the reign of Queen

Seventeenth-century gunpowder mill on the outskirts of Faversham

Opposite Near Oare

Elizabeth I. In 1914 there were four factories on the Uplees Marshes, and on 2 April 1916 an explosion killed more than a hundred people, seventy of whom were buried in a mass grave. Thousands of women workers were known as the Girls with Yellow Hands, through handling nitric oxide in the manufacture of TNT. The work was hard, but Faversham was prosperous during those days.

In 1916, because of the long walk in bad weather to the marsh factories two miles away, it was decided to lay down a light railway. This was opened in November of that year. Men and women travelled separately to work, women using later trains in the morning and getting away first in the afternoon so that they could attend to their home duties as well.

In 1915 four anti-aircraft guns were mounted to defend the powder works. A single German aeroplane dropped five bombs which fell in open fields. In 1917 the powder works had a narrow escape when four high-explosive bombs buried themselves in mud close to the factory. Three people were injured by the last German Gotha attack in 1918.

After the war the works were closed down. The buildings had been separated from each other, so an explosion in one would not trigger off a blast in any nearby, and such was their strength that much of the material earlier manufactured in them had to be used for their demolition.

I walk along the shore, and inland see a few concrete huts, and a rusting flat car in the fields. Otherwise the remains look like those of an ancient city. Some foundations are visible, the occasional fallen wall of concrete, and a huge iron mooring ring on the sea wall. The canals along which the powder punts were floated to the wharves are still distinct and filled with water. Otherwise it is an isolated stretch of marsh, with scores of sheep like inanimate white blobs on the green.

The area is as redolent of the Great War as are the trenches in France and Flanders. In such places the marks will never be erased. Great War songs still common in my childhood come back to me as I walk by the disused jetties. More than half of the workers were women, and no doubt the Gunpowder Girls, or the Girls with Yellow Hands, sang their songs which sounded across the marshes, tunes joined by the wind and swallowed by it:

We ride the train
In wind and rain:
It's more like a trolley
But we don't complain!

At Uplees Mills
And in Guncotton Folly
Sing Alice and Alma
And Ivy and Dolly –

Our wages are good
And the work isn't harsh
But our hands go yellow
On Gunpowder Marsh.

Though the vicar once told us
We ought not to sin,
We might drink beer
But we *never* drink gin.

On Sunday we walk
On Whitstable sands
Eating chips
From each other's hands.

Is there any young soldier
Who'll tip us a wink?
If we find such a lad
We'll buy him a drink.

For our young men we fight
And we don't shirk
From the wind and the rain
And the stink and the work.

At Uplees Mills
And in Guncotton Folly
Sing Alice and Alma
And Ivy and Dolly.

An R AF fighter comes in from the sea and goes across low, as if in salute. It is like walking through a dead city. A dock at Harty Ferry, where barges tied up for their cargoes of powder and guncotton, has the remains of light-railway tracks alongside. Between the sea wall and low waterline are fields of seakale and samphire, yellow flowers and green weeds with patches of dull water between. Many small boats are moored, and sheep graze on the ground plan of the powder works.

On these desolate marshes an attempt was made in 1551 to waylay Arden of Faversham; but he was saved by the timely descent of a fog. Arden's wife Alice, 'Young, tall, and well-favoured of shape and countenance' according to Hollinshed, had been seduced by a 'Black, swart serving-man called Mosbie' – a one-time tailor who induced two villainous sea-pirates to plot the husband's murder. One was Green of Faversham, and the other Black Will, 'a terrible cruel ruffian' who had acquired much evil experience during the French wars.

Harty Ferry

The play on this melancholy tale has been attributed to Marlowe and Shakespeare. After the Dissolution, when the lands of Faversham Abbey devolved on to 'Arden of Faversham', he turned a widow off her few acres, and those who knew of it ascribed his fate to her, for she cursed him roundly for such hardness of heart.

Mosbie's cronies also attempted to waylay Arden on Rainham Hill, but this too came to nothing. The plot needed more preparation before it could be effective. One Sunday evening Black Will hid himself in a closet in Arden's parlour, and when Arden sat down at suppertime to play a game with Mosbie, Green stood behind him with a candle in his hand to shadow Black Will as he appeared from his hiding place at the agreed signal.

Black Will came out and twisted a towel around Arden's neck, almost strangling him, but Mosbie finished him off. Outside it began to snow, and they carried the body to a garden house. When Alice came in she stabbed at the chest seven or eight times, then sent for a company of Londoners who were on a visit to Faversham, inviting them to 'sup and make merry, play, dance and sing'. When they had gone, the corpse 'in his night gown, and with his slippers on' was taken to a nearby field, and Alice went out to cry in the town that her husband had been murdered.

The mayor and others found the body in the croft. Some rushes of the sort that lay on the floor of Faversham's house were attached to it, and telltale footsteps in the snow led them to charge Alice with the murder, at which she became conscience-stricken: 'Oh, the blood of God help! For this blood have I shed!'

She was burned at the stake in Canterbury. Mosbie was hanged at Smithfield, and Green at Faversham. Black Will was captured some years later, and burned alive at Flushing.

Oare Creek, the main entrance to Faversham Fort, is signified by a boat skeleton wedged in the mud. Harty Cottages to the right are close to a site on which a battery of guns was once mounted to command both the creek and the Swale. Cows are in the field, and a line of pylons goes over the 20-metre height of Normans Hill. The slightest hump is a prominence in these parts. I fork left on a short cut to the village, hoping to find a shop and something to drink, but though I reach the road through various appendages to a farm, the final fence defeats me, especially as it is in full view of the parlour window and will probably break if I try to climb over. So I retreat back to the public track.

The village of Oare is named after the sea wrack which was collected

Opposite Oare Creek

along the shore, being Old English for seaweed: *wár*. The growing plant was cut from the rocks, dried, then burnt to make cinder ash or kelp for potters. The burning was done in holes dug on the beach, and so vile was the smell that the practice was forbidden by Queen Elizabeth on the ground that it was bad for the health of people who lived round about.

Oare stands on a hill across the meadows. A Dutchman at the entrance to the village asks if I know where he can hire a boat and boatman to take him to a point off the coast of Sheppey so that he can photograph a broadcasting station there. The tide is out and no boat will be able to leave for an hour or two, I tell him, by when it will be too late to photograph anything at all. The village seems to be asleep, so he gives up his quest, saying he will come back next year. He roars off on his 650 motorbike to get a meal in Faversham, and I walk up the other side of Oare Creek to marvel at the names of small boats moored there: *Alegre*, *Sabre Dance*, *Cimarron*, *Whimsby*, *Windrover*, *Dauntless*, *Emaro*, *May Maid*. There must be scores of thousands of such craft in every creek and inlet of Britain, owned by people wanting to escape their working lives and get onto the water.

By the Shipwrights' Arms, at the apex of Oare and Faversham creeks, is an ancient vessel called the *Orinoco* which, from its gaudy but fitting paintwork, looks as if it might have been up that river in its earlier days.

The beautiful and unspoiled banks of Faversham Creek make a nineteenth-century picture. Most guidebooks refer to 'this dreary shore', 'more grotesque than picturesque. The outskirts of Faversham are featureless' or 'A picturesque if rather melancholy quarter'.

The cattle meadows of Ham Marshes and old ships at the wharf, with their traditional barge masts and red rusty sails furled, create an ageless scene. One barge is the *Scotsman*. The *Ironsides* has a dog on deck too sleepy to repel even a cat, though alert for one all the same. Children play in a stream nearby, then it is so quiet that I hear the cough of an infant from the cabin of a smaller craft.

The peculiar tower of Faversham church beckons from the marshes, yet never seems to get closer, until suddenly it is out of sight and I am in the streets of the town and looking for the Ship Hotel. There is a room for me there, and soon afterwards I sit down to a dining-room supper of lamb chops, potatoes and peas, followed by a piece of opulent pie and a pot of strong tea.

The hotel is listed in most guidebooks as a notable building. The eighteenth-century front conceals an older structure, and there is a room

The *Orinoco* at Hollow Shore

upstairs – soon to be a residents' lounge, I was told by a waitress who showed it to me – where the thin ribs of the ceiling make a network of hexagons and date from the late sixteenth century. The hotel, well adapted, as Baedeker would say, for a stay of some time, is also a centre for local businessmen to meet and eat.

The family who run it resurrected it from the doldrums over two years ago. The dining room at that time was full of pintable machines, and served as a gathering place for the local skinheads. New rooms with showers are being put in, to give more sophisticated accommodation (though there was nothing lacking in my bedroom and breakfast, for £10.30). One is looked after in a homely and old-fashioned way, and the street on which the hotel stands has no motor traffic, which is a real boon to tired travellers.

Chapter Five

Faversham to Herne Bay

If I had been a little more knowledgeable when the young schoolteacher asked what Faversham was famous for, I would have mentioned beer as well as gunpowder. There are two breweries in town and, in a favourable wind (or otherwise, according to your predilections), the air reeks of hops and yeast. Perhaps it is no accident that the town stands to one side of the Roman highway going from Dover to Wroxeter, for otherwise, such is the quality of its ale (I know from experience) that no one would have got to London sober, or landed in France at all. The smell is at times so thick it seems you can almost live off it.

Apart from beer and the extinct gunpowder industry, Faversham is one of the most interesting and attractive towns in Kent. The place not only has architectural style, it has pubs. Some are next door to each other, and occasionally stand face to face across the street. One bears a sign saying VERY FINE VICTUALS, and I have no reason to doubt its truth when I see someone emerge at half past ten with clenched fists but a beautiful smile. What has been going on in there is not easy to say, but it must surely have been the stuff that stories are made of, judging by the fact that a sultry and good-looking girl comes out after him, takes his arm, and walks up the street giving him loving punches on the back. I won't say either of them were drunk. Probably no one in Faversham ever gets half seas over, especially if born there. They breathe hops and malt at the first gulp of mother's milk.

Two young men in the saloon bar of the Ship Hotel talk about their wages, and one says he worked fifty-six hours last week at £2.30 an hour, while the other admits that £128 was marked on his payslip, but then spits venom at the fact that his take-home pay is vastly different. He is so rattled at the amount of tax that he cannot say what it was. It seems, however, that there is sufficient money left for him to have a good time.

Faversham is a port of sorts, and has its industries, as well as a good secondhand bookshop; but the firmest impression comes from the homogeneity of its buildings. I want to get inside the church whose curious tower beckoned me in from the marshes, hoping to see the Early English frescoes 'relieved from superfluous whitewash during recent restorations' as one guidebook says (1872), in which 'the Jewish women are depicted in costumes which would have considerably astonished their contemporaries'. In what way? I wonder, though my curiosity can't be satisfied, because the doors are locked.

Nor could I inspect the early sixteenth-century timber-framed house built for the luckless (if stingy) Arden of Faversham, and in which he was, as the phrase goes, foully murdered. Another, though less serious, crime tells of how the Faversham fishermen were damned to eternity by the hapless James II, for preventing his escape in a small vessel lying at Shell Ness. They took his money and his watch, but not the diamonds, which they thought were bits of glass. He was then imprisoned in the Queen's Arms at Faversham, but afterwards moved to the mayor's house. He was so indignant at his rough treatment that when he issued a general amnesty

The Guildhall, Faversham

in 1692, he specifically excluded the fishermen of Faversham who had looted his pockets.

The town, unlike Rye, is not crowded with tourists, and is delightful to walk about in. It is an associate member of the Cinque Ports, while Rye is fully honoured in that company. It is on the flat, while Rye is hill-bound. Rye was burnt by the French, while Faversham was not. Cobbett called it 'a very pretty little town' – which it certainly is, and getting even more so because much restoration is being done.

It is no use repeating the author of the Kent volumes in the Buildings of England series, who calls Faversham 'one of the most rewarding towns in the county'. His perambulation through the streets makes the book essential. One visit which must be made is to the Fleur de Lys Museum on Preston Street, in which Faversham's past is agreeably laid out in maps, drawings, photographs, and objects both domestic and industrial. The interior is as small and intimate as it must be in many houses of the town. There is a slide show just off the entrance, and such a collection of books, pamphlets and postcards on sale concerning that part of Kent that I found it impossible to depart without spending a few pounds.

Even the railway station is a gem, with its yellow and red bricks, and the upside-down crenellated woodwork along its platforms. On a bench outside the ticket office, I hear two men tell each other they were seventy-seven years of age, at which one of them comments: 'How time do fly!'

It does, and I must leave for the 15-mile stretch to Herne Bay, first passing market stalls between the legs of the octagonal-shaped columns of the guildhall. At the end of Abbey Street I turn onto the creek side of quays and warehouses. PREVENTION OF RABIES, a notice says. NO ANIMALS MAY BE LANDED FROM ABROAD. It is early, and the smell of purifying dew holds down noise and distance. Visibility is barely two hundred yards. Grasses are beady with moisture. I pass the inevitable sewage works. Birds are subdued, but obvious. A tree spreading in the mist houses a rookery – a veritable Naples of a tree. The noise is deafening, as if the mist is a lid making it impossible for the birds to take off, holding them in by force. They fly suddenly while I pass underneath, and then there is silence, but for the rush of wings which I can't see.

Opposite Nagden Marshes

By Nagden Farm burnt stubble smells like potatoes in their jackets too long cooked. Gulls by the river, under cubic layers of mist, scream with the intensity of pigs being butchered. Lack of visibility upsets them, for they can see neither predators nor usurpers, which makes life twice as worrying. The area is a nature reserve, the marsh open to all comers.

Hammers clang in a boatyard across the creek, a mysterious pounding of metal from moored boats. None can be seen. The sound of a train comes from miles away, the mist most intense in the hour before it clears. The air is cool and warm at the same time. Human voices argue, but not clearly enough for me to make sense from their phrases.

Nettles are shoulder high along the sea-wall path. Yellow flowers of equal height take their place, till they are mixed up together, still dripping wet, saturating my trousers from the knees down. There is a three-foot concrete wall to my left, then lonely groynes poking out from the beach with no sign of water.

A man and a woman sit by a groyne, earnestly talking. The tide is out, mud for miles. Their low voices make it impossible to hear what is being said. They face each other and don't see me, yet speak as if not wanting to be overheard, sitting without coats or obvious provisions, as if they have stepped from their house to have a talk in the garden so as not to be overheard by the children.

The mist holds the world firmly down. Someone has aerosolled a white HELLO! on the wall. A soaked pyjama top hangs on a gate. Human voices far off on the mud shout to each other, but no one can be seen. When the tide is out there is dry sand as far as the South Oaze, and visibility can't be more than three hundred yards.

Sun shines over the land, and it is hot. Mist clears sufficiently for me to see four dim figures digging for something in the sand.

Nagden Marshes

At half past eleven I am back among chalets, bathing huts, caravans, bungalows and car parks, and passing Ye Old Sportsman pub. There are people on the beach and cattle in the fields. Cyclists and motorcars go along the road. Directly south, several miles away and over the summit of Clay Hill, yet sufficiently close to the Saxon Shore track to merit some reference, is a place where the Battle of Bossenden Wood occurred in 1838.

The main player in this tragic tale is John Nichols Thom, or Thorne, a tall and handsome man with a remarkable gift of natural eloquence. He was said to have been 'of humble birth' but was in fact the son of an innkeeper and small farmer of St Columb in Cornwall. More than one member of his family had shown signs of insanity. He was also said to have been of weak moral character, though many commented on his resemblance to the traditional representations of Jesus of Nazareth. Unfortunately, some people told him so, which did not improve the disorder of his wits.

Dressing himself with extravagant magnificence, he claimed to be Sir William Honeywood Courtnay, a Knight of Malta and heir to the Earldom of Devon, and to have been unjustly deprived of estates in that county. In London he masqueraded under many names, including that of Count Moses Rothschild, using the title to persuade many Jews to give him money on the pretext that he would use it to improve the condition of their co-religionists in Jerusalem.

He early on made a name as a swindler, seducer, impostor and arsonist. Being about thirty-five years old, he told people, with swaggering self-confidence, that his real age was 2000 years. Just above middle height, he was broad-shouldered and muscular, with dark hair parted in the middle and descending behind in long ringlets. His black beard and whiskers were set off by a superb dress of crimson velvet, gold facings, tassels and epaulettes. Anyone who interrupted his haranguing was threatened with the sword he carried.

In 1833 he stood for Parliament in Canterbury, and actually polled 960 votes; but at the end of that year certain transactions caused him to be convicted of perjury, to do with a trial of smugglers, and he was sentenced to three months' imprisonment, to be followed by six years' transportation. But before his jail term came to an end he was taken from Maidstone and sent to the county lunatic asylum where, considered to be mad, he remained four years. In August 1837 his parents brought pressure to bear on Lord John Russell, the Home Secretary, who humanely but foolishly caused him to be released in the spring of 1838. His parents took no steps to look after him, and he was again on the loose.

At the end of May 1838 he was living at Bossenden Farm and, reappearing in his old haunts, proclaimed himself to be the Messiah. In this guise he attracted a certain following and his influence spread not only among ignorant peasants, but also among the respectable farmers. As the extent of Thorne's madness grew, so did the number of his followers. He gave out that he was impervious to swords and bullets and, in the flowering of his Mad Mullah-like delusions, claimed to be able to work miracles, assuring his followers that if they remained loyal they would become equally invulnerable.

One of the farmers complained however that his workers were being enticed away by Thorne. On 28 May 1838 Thorne led a hundred partly armed adherents through several villages. At Durgate Common he took off his shoes and proclaimed that the ground he stood on was now holy, and would be for ever so. His band fell on their knees and prayed.

They slept in Bossenden Wood, and next day visited a further six villages, covering a distance of 17 miles. He preached a communistic doctrine from his white horse, as well as insisting that he was the Messiah. The emblem of his followers was a pole stuck through a loaf of bread. Thorne said he would lead them to glory and share all landed estates among them so that each would get fifty acres.

On 30 May they returned to Bossenden Wood. A warrant had been issued against him, and three constables, two of whom were brothers by the name of Mears, went to the farm on 31 May to bring him in.

Thorne rushed out of the doorway – after a short parley – and shot one of the constables dead. The others ran for their lives when he attacked them with a sword. He then hacked at the body of the dead man and told his followers to sling it into a ditch, crying out: 'Now am I not your Saviour?'

After a mock absolution and administration of the sacrament, he said that the weapons of the soldiers who would now be brought against them would be powerless.

The two uninjured constables reported to the magistrates, and when the news reached Canterbury it was considered that the matter now called for drastic action.

Early that year the 45th Regiment of Foot (Sherwood Foresters) had marched from Gravesend to barracks in Canterbury. The officer commanding was ordered to send two companies, made up of a hundred rifles, to Bossenden Wood. Major Armstrong was in charge, and had with him Captain J. Reid and Lieutenants T. Prendergast and H. B. Bennett.

Bossenden Wood extended for about twelve hundred yards from north to south, and five hundred from east to west, the farmhouse being situated in a narrow clearing on the east side. To the east was another large wood, 2 miles in extent, thus giving plenty of cover, and room for the rebels to manoeuvre. They retreated to a deep and sequestered part and, while waiting for the inevitable attack, were worked into a state of desperate fury by Thorne's harangues.

Major Armstrong divided his detachment into two parties. One commanded by Captain Reid was to move up a lane to Bossenden Farm, while Armstrong himself came by the Faversham road and turned north along the western edge of the wood. Thus both parties entered the wood from opposite sides, and found the rioters practically at the same time. One of Thorne's followers held up a large white flag with a blue border, and a gold lion rampant in the middle.

Lieutenant Bennett went towards the leader and called on him to surrender. Thorne came out of the rough stockade to meet him and, before anyone was aware of his intention, shot the twenty-nine-year-old Bennett dead. The Sherwood Foresters fired a volley, and Thorne fell mortally wounded, shouting before he died: 'I have Jesus in my heart!'

The rioters advanced en masse against the soldiers with cudgels and pitchforks. The Sherwood Foresters fixed bayonets, and in a short time the rioters were dispersed, ten being killed, seven wounded and twenty-five made prisoner. The Sherwood Foresters' casualties of three killed and one wounded did not constitute a battle honour to be incorporated in their cap badge, but *The Times* newspaper commented:

It is only just to this Regiment, which from its recent return from India is now composed pretty generally of young recruits, to state that the men ordered out on this occasion conducted themselves with great steadiness and temper, and ceased firing immediately on hearing the signal to that effect. There were not more than sixty shots fired, but by those sixty, ten were killed and as many more wounded.

When the inquest took place, in the parlour of the Lion Inn, women gathered with bits of oak bark pulled from the tree against which Thorne had staggered when shot. Thousands came to see him in his coffin, as if their Messiah might rise again and lead them once more.

The wailing of mourners sounded from many houses, for the villagers were nearly all related to the dead rioters through intermarriage. The burial service took two hours, amid great sorrow and grief. Liberal people afterwards started education schemes for the area, appalled that such bigotry had been able to take hold in a civilized country.

After arranging for a memorial tablet to be put up in Canterbury Cathedral for Lieutenant Bennett, the regiment was sent to Newport in Monmouthshire, and there distinguished itself further by shooting dead twenty Chartist rioters and wounding dozens more. India had apparently been a good school, although it must be said that of the Newport firing party only three men were over twenty-three years of age.

Children play happily on the beach. I pass catamarans with such names as *Thor*, *Abu* and *Camilla*, then lines of tied-up sailing boats. The straggling settlement of Seasalter is as if coated into silence by the mist. The place takes its name from salt pans which once existed on the shore. In 1953 exceptionally high tides inundated the area, and the sea wall on which I walk was built afterwards as a rampart.

One can motor through a place and see nothing of it, cycle through and recall very little, but a place you walk through can never be forgotten. The sun gives glamour, the rain gloom, and the mist mystery, and I sit by a groyne on the stony beach to eat lunch, glad that out of the three there is no rain.

Competitors in the Swale Sailing Barge and Fishing Smack Race

The footpath parallels a road through the Granville Cliffe Estate, with notices at the entrance saying PRIVATE. ACCESS FOR RESIDENTS ONLY. NO PARKING. PLEASE KEEP TO THE FOOTPATH. I think that while they were about it they might have added NO HAWKERS OR CIRCULARS. NO COACHES. NO TRIPPERS. NO PROLES. NO CHILDREN. NO COCKNEYS. NO GYPSIES. NO LABOUR VOTERS. NO BLACKS. NO HUNGER MARCHERS.

I am soon out of it, over a railway bridge and onto an ordinary street with a couple of pubs. There are 7 miles of built-up area, which is not unattractive, because the sea is either visible between houses or colourfully obvious.

The route leads downhill to a common area of bushes and footpaths where dogs are walked, then over a railway footbridge and on a raised path across a golf course, finally getting back to a strand lined with bathing huts. The sun is out but the sea stays misty, casting a pleasant sheen over beach houses, reminiscent of the French Channel coast.

With so many boats, chalets, parked cars and the occasional opulent bungalow, I think what fun the Saxon berserkers such as Sweyne Forkbeard and Eric the Bloodaxe might have if by some warp of time they were able to land here. Yet if by a similar warp machine guns were employed to hold them off, maybe the gala wouldn't be all one-sided.

It is a coast of squash clubs, and happy families going to the beach, and the place is by no means crowded for late summer. Even the huts don't blemish the locality, and the shingle has only a few discreet ripples of sea hissing against it. A huge flat surfboard with a sail coloured yellow, orange and green skims in and out of sight. The path is a paved sea walk, easy on the feet, and my army boots clop comfortably along.

Whitstable High Street and Western Harbour Street extension make a quaint thoroughfare, with plenty of antique shops selling all kinds of enticing gewgaws. They are fortunately closed for lunch, or I might be tempted to rummage among the boxes and shelves. The window of an open patisserie is also interesting: to eat and drink frequently is the secret of prolonged walking, and I try never to miss a supply point without taking advantage of it.

Whitstable has about 25,000 inhabitants, ten times the number of a hundred years ago. There are some attractive weatherboard cottages near the shore, and many late visitors give the place a holiday atmosphere.

For two thousand years its oysters have been famous. In the days of Juvenal they found their way to Nero's Golden House and Domitian's Alban Villa. Whether they are still cultivated I don't know, but one company of the Free Fishers and Dredgers was incorporated as long ago as 1793. The area of the beds covers nearly 5000 acres and begins about 2 miles off shore, extending for more than 7 miles. In the middle of the nineteenth century, a certain Mr Alston sent in a single year more than 50,000 bushels to London from his fishery at Cheyney Rock near Sheerness. Lord Kitchener was exceedingly fond of them, and Shakespeare swallowed them at 1s 4d a hundred. They were said to sharpen the wits, and other things, wonderfully.

Whitstable's courageous divers visited every part of the coast to recover valuable cargo from wrecks. Pilgrims for Canterbury came ashore here, and the first passenger railway in England was opened between the two places in May 1830, when the trucks also carried coal from the barges at Whitstable for distribution all over Kent.

Opposite Whitstable

Whitstable

Opposite 'Daydreams', Whitstable

On the outskirts of Whitstable an old woman in a wheelchair is being persuaded by her stout bespectacled keeper that it is time to get back into the car a few yards away. But the old lady doesn't want to leave the beach. She looks ancient and fractious, as if she might die if put into a temper. She is obstinate and doesn't care to move. To stay and witness the end of the conflict would be a rude violation, so I go on my way.

The tide is coming in, and more men are fishing from the groynes. Hundreds of chalets line the route, looking like second homes, or seaside *dachas*. Some have doors open, and people eat or sunbathe outside. Daumier should have come sketching here. Chalets have names like Osmunda, The Shingles, and Yamba. Two Irish nuns talk to each other from their deckchairs.

By another hut I see a man mending a split in a rubber boat with Sellotape. He is about forty, sober, intent, though also pugnacious, as if a fight might result if I politely told him not to be so daft. He carefully pulls the tape loose and binds it across the wound, over and over, while a boy and girl look on trustingly and with admiration at his being so clever as to mend their boat. Daddy can do anything. No trouble is too much. He has given up his nap, or his newspaper, or both, to be their hero yet again, this time to mend the rubber boat with Sellotape so that they can play happily in the gentle but misty sea. Dear Daddy with his Sellotape. What a brainwave to think of it. I hope to God Mummy comes back and screams at him.

Visibility varies, five hundred yards one minute, a mile the next. The island end of Herne Bay pier is like Xanadu in the mist, an illusive cake-like White House stranded in the sea. The original pier, built at enormous cost by Telford in 1832, was constructed entirely of wood. The teredo worm made a delectable meal of the prime timber and eventually destroyed it. The first pile of the present jetty was screwed into place in 1896, and opened for people three years later, an additional pavilion being added in 1908.

The octagonal pavilion can only be reached by boat, being three-quarters of a mile from shore and the connecting links having been washed away in a storm. An electric tram once ran along the pier, and before that trucks were driven by sails hoisted in the wind.

88/*Faversham to Herne Bay*

Closer to the pierhead are more arcades, ice-cream parlours, bingo rooms, cafés, roller-skating rinks, and children's playgrounds. The pierhead pavilion looks like an aircraft repair workshop, corrugated and grey. A row of tots on a trampoline are going up and down like bottles of liqueur.

Even fifty years after the pier has been swept away, people congregate at the space in front, and a performance by morris dancers is about to begin. They are mostly men, in black top hats, some flowered, others feathered. They wear black trousers and stockings with buckles, and white shirts with black overlays marked by yellow crosses. One or two girls have on floral peasant costumes, and when the dance master announces, in a voice that must shiver timbers as far as Tankerton, that the next dance is to be (in honour of the recent royal wedding) 'The Princess Royal', a ripple of clapping comes from the semicircle of trippers.

Accordions, concertinas and the big drum begin their music, a mixture of shipboard stuff and English bucolic. Sailors with wooden legs and harrowed faces once watched. With great energy the dancers go up in two columns, come close and clack hands, then move outwards and round, and back again (after sundry circles) in a line to face each other, and stamp out their geometry and pump at their music with great energy and aplomb – English music sounding in mysterious English air, making England seem at the moment a place for possible adventure and pleasant surprise.

Welcome to Herne Bay. I make my way through quiet streets towards the garden of remembrance and the railway station. All jollity happens at the pierhead and along the promenade, while at sea the old pavilion glows like a temple made out of lardy cake.

Opposite The Street, Whitstable

Chapter Six
Along the Wantsum

As far as I can tell, and I had a good search, there are no secondhand bookshops in Herne Bay. There isn't even a bay, though the front certainly occupies a fine position on the coast. I expect that when the town's quiet, which must be for most of the year, it's very very quiet, but when it's noisy there's only a moderate rockiness in the air. The climate, as the guidebooks say, is delightful and bracing, and though I often question whether the two are synonymous, Herne Bay beats all other seaside resorts when it comes to the number of sunny hours in the year. The low death rate has more than once been commented on with enthusiasm by the Registrar General, but not, I suspect, by the undertakers.

I look on the map for the bay, and see no evidence. Gazing out to sea on either side of the pier, I cannot make out the semblance of an indentation. A seaside resort has to assert one false claim, otherwise no one will believe the others.

Herne Bay, invented as a watering place in 1830, was for years a wilderness of uncompleted houses and half-laid-out streets, involving speculators in litigation and ruin. Such days are long past and, on the surface at least, Herne Bay is as staid a place as can be found anywhere.

Bungalow development goes back from the sea as far as the station, while substantial houses and older streets are closer to the front. On Sunday morning one or two milk floats turn corners, and the occasional newspaper boy rides by. A sort of prefabricated Kingdom Hall of the Jehovah's Witnesses on one side of the road is faced by a funeral parlour.

The twin towers of Reculver are sharp and plain to the east. Weather is dry but the sky is overcast. A pub called the Four Fathoms causes me to wonder why only four. The tide is out, the grey sea relatively calm. Warden Point is in clear view 10 miles away, as well as forts, ships and a few boats. The end of the pier which looked so dreamlike on approaching

At Herne Bay most of the pier has fallen into the sea

from Whitstable is a very small and squalid pergola with a Russian onion dome coming to a point and suggesting a kind of covered-in bandstand. Herne Bay in fact is a perfect late-nineteenth-century bandstand town, where people of the so-called better class came on holiday and listened to the band thumping away.

East along the front at half past nine, I pass a miniature children's railway, the same old wooden Puffing Billies and Teddy Bear carriages. There is a clock-golf course, a clock tower, poster illuminations, Leisureland, the gift shop, a central-heating supply shop, a restaurant called the Seagull, the Divers' Arms, bingo hall, kebab house, Golden Guinea Amusement Arcade, Talk of the Town Show, coffee bar and ice-cream parlour. A few people already play space games with appropriate noises and flashing lights. Sherwood Court Hotel is a home for the elderly. There is a British Legion branch. The Department of Health and Social Security is a five-storey house with handsome steps and a notice which spoils it all, saying: ENTRANCE AT THE REAR, IN CHARLES STREET.

There is a break in the clouds, and pleasurably good visibility. A squalid set of detached cottages, with white pebble-dash fronts and black windowframes, is followed by an intriguing Alhambra-style cafeteria called Kings Hall, with slender pillars, arabesque arches and fancy railing work along the flat roof.

Reculver Abbey

Outside Herne Bay sailing club, by a line of canvas-covered boats, is a catamaran called *The Six Million Dollar Machine*. The cement pathway goes along the groyned pebble beach. To the right is sloping grassland, with the houses of Beltinge beyond. The twin towers of Reculver church, set on a jutting cliff in the distance, give reality to the present shabbiness.

Two seafaring men in jerseys and caps are exercising three black muscular dogs. A church bell tolls some way off – but not for me – seeming to ricochet from an ominous circumvallation of cloud that hems in the white middle of the sun. A neatly thatched cottage stands on a ridge, and out on the tidal mud a grey-haired man with a rucksack is looking for limpets. Sunday morning is a world of its own.

Buoys and beacons mark the channel. A short detour inland threads Chaletville to avoid the gully of Bishopstone Gap, going along a muddy path through trees. I resume the reddish soil of the footpath, which here shows off the finest section of Lower Tertiary deposits in England. Paleolithic gravel forms the top of the cliff, with a basement bed of London clay.

There are sharp inlets into the overhang, as if a monster has now and again come up from the sea and taken enormous bites out of the shore. People walk their dogs. A man-wife-and-two-kids with all kinds of bucket-and-spade combinations, as well as picnic paraphernalia, file down to the beach. Reculver, like Jerusalem, never seems to get any nearer. Buildings of Margate crowd the coast ahead. From the prefabricated structure of the coastguard lookout post a series of bearings tells me that the power station to the southeast is Richborough, 14 kilometres away.

Steamers, fishing boats, cargo ships and tankers are around the jut of North Foreland. The grass pathway is pleasant to walk on. Cabbage fields stretch beyond the green track. A father and two sons ride suitably proportioned bikes along the grassy path, a Sunday morning verve in their manoeuvres. Rover runs in front, a frolicking advance guard reconnoitering the route, making great circles and loxodromes as he homes back out

towards them. On a more exuberant track he stops a mere few inches from the cliff edge, sniffing disaster with his direction-finding nose, at which he spins, and hares rapidly inland, then goes forward to make the world safe for his sluggishly advancing bikes. He is the mainstay and pace-setter of mankind.

A red anorak bends intently, harvesting the sea mud, puts something into its mouth, but whether sweet or limpet I'll never know. A notice near Reculver says: PERSONS ARE ADVISED THAT SHELLFISH GATHERED FROM THE FORESHORE MUST BE BOILED THOROUGHLY BEFORE CONSUMPTION.

Reculver is surrounded by caravan parks – Caravanville with a vengeance. Over a stile and between two fences I hope no calor-gas bottle outside each tethered living van will explode, because if one does, so will the next, and I will clearly regret not being alive by the end to have witnessed a spectacular example of the domino theory in practice.

Reculver's ruined church is on the site of the Roman fort of Regulbium, one of the defences of the Saxon Shore built in the third century of the Common Era to guard the northern entrance of the straits which divided the Isle of Thanet from the mainland. The fort at the southern entrance was Richborough, where the power station now is, 8 crow-miles away.

King Egbert of Kent founded a monastery here in 669. The twin towers, a landmark for mariners and walkers, were put up in the twelfth century. They are known as the Sisters – the legend saying that they were built by the Abbess of Davington to commemorate the death of her sister, and also as an offering of thanks for her own escape from drowning.

The story is that the abbess of the Benedictine nuns at Faversham became dangerously ill, and vowed that if she recovered she would visit the shrine of the Blessed Virgin at Bradstow, some miles along the coast, and present a costly offering.

She embarked on 3 May with her sister Isobel, for whom 'she entertained the warmest affection'. After two hours a storm broke, and drove the ship onto a sandbank near Reculver. Some of the crew and passengers, including the abbess, reached shore in a boat, but Isobel stayed in the wreck till a boat was sent to rescue her. She suffered much from cold and exhaustion, and died the following day. To perpetuate her memory, and to warn sailors of the dangerous coast, the abbess had the towers rebuilt and spires added.

A Roman city lies under the water, and the sea nibbles the shore at the rate of two feet a year. In 1805 Reculver church and village stood in safety, but the sea began to encroach and farmers sold the seaside stonework to the Margate Pier Company. In 1832 the chapelhouse fell, and the parishioners were permitted to demolish the church; but Trinity House intervened and restored the western portion as a landmark. Little of the village remains, and the one-time vicarage is now the Ethelbert Arms. In chalk on a piece of board nearby I read:

> Ethelbert and Ethelberta
> Gave shelter to a Danish deserter –
> They fed him beer and blood-red meat,
> Then killed him, and sat down to eat.

One of the coastguard cottages is falling into ruin, a large hole in the roof and all windows tinned up. The car park forbids dogs and touring vans. The Blue Dolphin Club advertises live music, with dancing and cabaret nightly. Caravans, amusement places, snackbars, ice-cream palaces and fish-and-chipboard shacks – a shanty city has risen from the soil to cater to the shellfish gold rush. The office of the Sunset Caravan Company Limited is signposted with a 5-mile-per-hour speed notice underneath. You go slowly into that goodnight.

South along a cornfield footpath, I feel no desire to look back at Bidonville-on-the-Wantsum, as the channel between Thanet and Kent is called. The hay is rolled into great round drums. I navigate by noise on hearing a train ratcheting along a line I am due to cross. I hope there are no bulls among the black and white cows, because a wide ditch is the only way of escape. My hand touches a rabbit petrified in the herbage, but I don't try to catch it because I can't kill something so obviously afraid.

At eleven the path goes under the railway, then along a concrete track ascending towards Chislet Mill:

> Chislet Windmill has no sails:
> I wonder where they flew?
> Perhaps the equinoctial gales
> Loosened nails and glue,
> Until each battered board got free
> And soared across the sea!

Stacks of hay are as big as small cottages. I pass through waterlogged cauliflower fields. There is heavy mud, pools of water, forlorn pigeons, sad doves and saturated vegetables.

The paved lane beyond Thanet Way looks a neglected cart track, due to potholes and mud. Farther on, macadam becomes more apparent. Wheat to the left and onions to the right. England is agriculturally wealthy. Industry may be smashed, but food production thrives, though it employs few men. I know a farmer who works six hundred acres with no more than three skilled men.

Fields are harvested, onions in heaps. The slight wind makes an agreeable walking temperature. Much shooting comes from the southwest. Off the paved lane, I go onto a mud track, still heading south. In sharp visibility, large bales of hay on a hilltop look like a Stonehenge of wheat silhouetted against thick grey cloud.

I skirt the hamlet of Boyden Gate by the backs of houses, by stile and stream and through fields, passing a gaggle of geese that honk till I am back at the lane, by which point it is midday, time to eat German sausage, rye bread and an apple, washed down by tea. It is cold standing still, so I light up for a smoke and get on the move.

Chitty Lane is a mere car width, with a green-coated ditch on either side because the land is now flat, though not cheerless. A blue plastic fertilizer bag, indestructible except by fire, lies among the bulrushes. A black Chitty cat with green eyes stares, then runs into the hedge with – I swear – a grin as if it has done me irreparable harm.

A rookery sounds as if a fox has got up into the tree. The muddy track goes through a scrap of wood. Fields are burnt, as if the Danes have been and gone. Chislet's Norman church to the right looks as if its steeple has fallen off at some time or other.

Along a rough grassy track I spot a solitary stem of reddish-purple clover, of which there seems nothing else similar for miles. In a field of cows, a bull trots towards me. I turn and face him. He stops, too, twenty feet away. I walk towards a gate. He follows, but less quickly. I am not afraid, but cautious. My farrier grandfather had ringed young bulls, a cruel trade – as one of his daughters put it. He pierced the bull's nose to get a ring through, a terrible part of his anatomy to pain and disfigure. If it is true that the sins of the grandfather may be visited on the grandson, then I want to avoid any such apposite retribution, whatever idea the stalking bull may have.

When I think the bull is getting too close I turn again, and stare at him. The glitter in his eyes begins to wander, though the left hoof twitches. It is difficult to know whether the Saturn-like glitter shows his uncertainty, or whether it merely illustrates the various stages of his decision-making process. I walk a few more yards towards the gate. There is no escape should he charge. I'm in his field, not on a lane looking in.

I stop and turn, I talk in a loud voice, but forget the words as soon as I have spoken. They are soothing nevertheless, empty of flattery. He stops. I think that, above all, he is curious.

At the gate, I don't wait to unlatch and open it but, hearing the heavy trot, climb over and walk away, mud and straw underfoot jacking me a few inches closer to heaven.

I navigate by noise over the crest of a hill, hearing traffic along a road I must intersect. There is no evidence of a footpath so I use the compass, hoping I will reach the road to the left of Upstreet Farm. Gulls on the field are like little white flags on a golf course.

I cross the A28 near Upstreet a hundred metres off track, then through a burnt field with the shadow of a footpath which would look much clearer from the air. I get a glimpse of the Great Stour, with the inevitable lines of pleasure boats on its banks. I go over the slight rise of ground, having done the four waters by walking from the Thames to the Medway, to the Swale and to the Stour.

There are lines of cars outside Grove Ferry Inn and Sunday people crowding inside at the bars. The usual flashing lights and space-game noises compete with the latest jungle music. I get my pint and, though it is chill, sit outside.

Each garden table has four iron ornamental white chairs leaning inwards to denote they are not to be used. I pull one down and sit on it, and get a shaky seat because what looks like metal is in fact a plastic imitation, light and silent to move.

A car nearby has rusty holes along its bodywork big enough to push a fist in, but inside is the most expensive stereophonic system I've seen in a long time. One must admire the owner for knowing his (or her) priorities.

Every few yards along the riverbank there are old men, women, young men and women, and even groups of children casting their first lines, all quiet and intent as they fish away the day. Talk is a quick passing of advice and encouragement, and no more.

Crossing a field towards the Little Stour, there is an unutterable stench, which I can only attribute to the closing proximity of Pluck's Gutter. The sheep are tame, perhaps due to senses dimmed by the foul air they live in. They stare vacantly from two or three feet away – instead of running as soon as I get into the field.

A flight of seven huge swans with heads right forward and large wings

slowly flapping come up river. Level, they veer across the marsh like a
squadron of aeroplanes. The same huge cable drums of hay are in fields to
the right.

Plucks Gutter

I get used to the foul exhalations of Old Pluck's gutter. What a man Old
Pluck must be. There is in fact no apostrophe, so I make it plain Plucks
plural and envisage Mr and Mrs Pluck, a gross old pair who eat themselves
silly, and foul the air for miles around. No respectable pub or motorists'
roadhouse will have them inside its premises, so they are doomed to eat –
and especially drink – at home. And they do, God bless them – and though
they like their very fine victuals, they dote on each other as well, to the
extent of being totally unaware of the blight that their excesses cast over
the otherwise benign and pleasing countryside. If they walk, it is mostly at
night when they go arm in arm to the back door of the Dog and Duck with
a huge cloth bag each to get bottles of booze for their ongoing debauch.
Long may they live in peace and splendour.

I walk easterly, and pass apple orchards before coming to the aforesaid Gutter, where boats are again at their moorings, miniature cabin cruisers very old and rough, much loved but somewhat neglected. Eschewing the Dog and Duck, I walk under the bridge at Plucks Gutter, boats now fancier on the main arm of the river, though soon no more are moored and even fishermen don't venture this far from the road, and I am on my own, going on the good south bank path towards Richborough power station, over 4 miles away.

The empty quarter that stretches before me is one of the few extensive marshlands of southern England. Stile after stile and bridge after rickety bridge separates one field from another. All land once under water is now dyke-drained and rich for grazing. One branch of the Stour begins near Lenham, and the other, the East Stour, rises near Postling. They unite at Ashford and flow through parks and pasture to Canterbury, going on to Fordwich till joined by the Little Stour at Plucks Gutter. By Sandwich the Stour almost doubles back on itself, to debouch into the English Channel at Pegwell Bay.

The occasional well-appointed launch, or sailboat under power, comes up river. All have the Red Duster fluttering at the stern, even the smallest and humblest which looks as if it might sink at any minute. It seems appropriate that such an emblem be displayed on these sleepy yet disputable marshes, where the opulent bud of Thanet can be nipped off in one sharp meeting of an invader's pincer claws.

One boat has all hatches closed, and a bearded young skipper half dozes in his covered bridge, no doubt imagining himself captain of a large craft. Handsome but well-worn boats come drifting by, bound for some prearranged mooring by Plucks Gutter, which is as much the centre of the world on this day as is Jerusalem on the thirteenth-century map in Hereford Cathedral.

The world is at peace as I walk through fields of idle sheep and somnolent cows, the river a navigational highway giving longitude, while a compass bearing on Minster church completes the fix when I stop for tea: a map reference of 298629 at 1525 hours. Fifteen minutes later a pylon crosses the river, and so I calculate my rate of walking on that particular stretch to be 2.7 miles per hour.

I look for a building shown on the map as Providence Cottage, and think that if it exists, and if I were a Texan oil millionaire, and if David Mercer were still alive, which alas he is not, I would buy it for him, because he wrote a memorable film called *Providence*. Scouring the landscape when the cottage should have been four hundred yards due south, the place where it should stand now has a dozen or so cows gathered around zinc troughs at their water. Providence Cottage, like so much else in life, seems to have vanished, and an appropriate sadness is felt until it is dispelled by the sound of gunshots.

They come from lanes and houses to the south, sharply rippling the air, as if a homestead is under siege and a plucky group is holding out against great odds. I look through my binoculars, but see nothing. The firing grows to a crescendo. Perhaps one or several of the besieged are making a run for it. Or maybe the final rush of the place is being made, because they are a pack of vile terrorists within, who have murdered only the innocent. After that fusillade and a couple of final shots, there is silence. No prisoners taken. Perhaps it only means that the ducks can rest in peace, until the next exuberant firing party comes by.

I pass Boxlees Hill and Weatherless Hill – neither of them an obvious rise of ground. Hopes of a dry firm path all day are spoiled when at four o'clock I go back into the muddy jungle at the railway bridge. The water is clean and sandy in the middle. Under the bridge supports I crave a machete to get through the brambles and bushes, swampy encumbered

Richborough power station

inlets and tough reed grass. The hard going makes me sweat as I push the vegetation aside, legs lifting high to tread it down by every step.

The power station looms, and sinisterly hums on the opposite bank, working to full power but with not a man in sight, as if running only by malign computer. The three cooling towers have dominated much of the day's walk, and will no doubt follow me halfway through tomorrow. It was built in 1963, after the idea of making a car-ferry terminal had been abandoned.

The place was formerly the location of a Great War transport depot. In 1916 an army of 20,000 Royal Engineers set to work on the salt marshes between Sandwich and Pegwell Bay, widening and deepening to cut a navigable channel across the horseshoe bend of the Stour. Two hundred and fifty acres of swamp were drained, and a mile of wharves fitted with cranes, forming a camp and harbour covering 1500 acres.

Few knew of its existence till after the Great War, except the soldiers who left by it for France. Built to relieve traffic at Dover, guns and ammunition, railway and other war material went over the Channel on barges which travelled up the French canals, as close as they could get to

Richborough Castle

Richborough Castle and power station

the firing line before unloading. Later in the war it was developed as a train ferry, and for the conveyance of 700 tanks which were taken to the Western Front before the Armistice.

After the Great War the establishment was sold as an industrial estate; but during the Second World War it was used as a base for landing craft, and parts of the giant caissons for Mulberry Harbour were assembled before being towed to the Normandy invasion area in June 1944.

Nowadays the huge and magnificent power station seems as if it will be here for longer than any of those former enterprises, though I lose interest in its fate while struggling along the river, through brambles and ragwort. I also fail to mull on the many illustrious landings that have taken place at the mouth of the river near Ebbsfleet only a mile away – the traditional disembarkation point of the Saxons in 449, and of St Augustine in 597.

Stonar was, with Sandwich, one of the main seaports of London. Outward-bound vessels could take up their last passengers and provisions from either place, before steering into the open sea. The French burned Stonar down in 1385. A non-corporate member of the Cinque Ports, it returned briefly to glory as part of Richborough Port in 1916, and Stonar House was an RAF depot during the last war.

Jungle along the path thins and disappears, but otherwise the whole locality is laced with shit and mud, which seems to epitomize this part of England, at least as far as footpaths go. Bits of concrete are half buried in the path, as if pillboxes or former quays were blown up and scattered – not big pieces, but the boots catch on them, till I find a better alignment closer to the river bank. On the opposite side are storage huts remaining from two wars, all in good repair and well painted, though magazines and hangars farther on, which come right to the shore, are much shabbier.

The path is again encumbered with brambles, huge thistles, and all kinds of vegetation. Passing Stonar Cut, only a few more miles remain for Sandwich. Keeping as close as possible to a wire fence bordering a field makes it less difficult to get along. Between the power station and Sandwich are tips, works, breakers' yards and an enormous field of plastic bags, bits of old tyre, jerrycans and bottles, poking out of soil and ash, but as if someone had made a pathetic attempt to plough them in, but gave up on seeing that he was only disturbing more detritus underneath. A few thousand volunteers could close England's industrial wounds in a very short time. The marks of civilization have to be left somewhere, however, and perhaps it's better here than in most places.

By Richborough Castle the land returns to the picturesque, which means merely clean and tidy. Over the railway in the other direction the land is covered in dark woods of one-tone green, the afternoon flatland light making them seem very thick indeed.

In Roman times the hill and castle of Richborough was an island at the mouth of the Wantsum. The landing place of Aulus Plautius and his invading army in 43 of the Common Era, the camp became a supply depot during the conquest of southern England that followed, and then the chief port. In the fourth century, one of a chain of forts around the southeast coast, Richborough resisted the Saxons, and its commander was known as the Count of the Saxon Shore. The place flourished till abandoned by the Romans in the fifth century, and the massive thirty-foot walls that for a while intimidated the Saxons now stand out darkly. Just before the First World War sheep were pastured within the enclosure.

Turning left by the Canterbury road, I enter Sandwich at half past five. The walls ring the inner town, and a footpath goes along by a channel of

Sandwich water covered with green slime. The wall trackway is here called The Butts. To the left are town houses, and to the right a cricket match is being played, all contestants dressed in white. A few hundred years ago they would have been practising archery. The name of the path changes to The Ropewalk. After more than 18 miles, my feet ache, but I don't seem to have any blisters.

Chapter Seven
The Golf Coast

A house called The Drum stands next door to one labelled The Witches Brew. *Drum* is the one-time slang for 'bawdy house', but I don't imagine there is any connection. Other house names are Malt Shovel, Apple Tree Cottage, Clay Pipe, Delf House, Blenheim House, Old Forge, The Maltings – whole streets of seventeenth-century dwellings. On Bowling Street are houses called Pieces of Eight, Drake Cottage and Ninepins.

The High Street is not so by nature or purpose, for it has almost no shops and is pleasant to walk along on Monday morning, and reflect on how little Sandwich has altered since I was first here thirty years ago. The town is untouched by anything modern, and even the railway is placed well south of the ancient centre. A recent bypass has completed the peace, and on this sunny morning I hum the old folk songs as sung by Shirley Collins in the sixties.

Nevertheless, the place has had such violent ups and downs that it might easily have succumbed as did Pompeii to its rain of ash and clinker. Roman Rutupiae (Richborough) and Stonor, being of no further use to the sailors due to physical changes of the coastline, brought Sandwich into use. In both Danish invasions the struggle for the defence of England took place around Sandwich and nearby Estree. The Danes, displacing the Saxons, consolidated their conquests here, because Sandwich commanded the direct route to Canterbury and London. Canute landed in 1013, and when he became King of England rebuilt the town after its wartime tribulations.

A squadron of Danish pirates pillaged the town with great savagery during Edward the Confessor's reign, but it revived and, due to its strategic position, became the chief English port from which to conduct sea warfare between the Channel and the North Sea, and between the Continent and Britain. By the eleventh century the place was already a thriving Cinque Port. In 1216 it was burnt by the French. The Bohemian ambassador, who passed through in 1446, described the place as one might speak of Liverpool or Bristol in the nineteenth century.

In 1456, Marshal de Brezé landed with 4000 men, burnt the town and killed nearly all the inhabitants. In 1588 it played a great part in providing ships and men to keep the Spanish armada from the shores of England. Flemish refugees, fleeing Spanish tyranny, reinvigorated the declining town. Five hundred of them manufactured beige, serge and flannel, and from their extensive market gardens in the environs produced a notable species of celery.

But the decline was endemic, and perhaps the only universal item which will perpetuate the name of the place was when the First Lord of the Admiralty, the patron of Captain Cook, the Navigator, invented sandwiches. It was not until the nineteenth century that the game of golf gave it back some renown, and a little prosperity.

The history of all such places is one of alternating ravagement and riches. Survival depends on good harvests, mercantile success, training for warfare, and tactical ingenuity in defeating attacks by marauders. The marauders themselves, in the grip of shortage, are driven to thriving places to improve themselves by pillage, and gain a momentary respite from misery by vandalistic enjoyment. To those people killed and plundered, it seems like an act of God. The plunderers do not enjoy their gains for long. Only industry furthers, and vigorous self-defence which in order to be effective must also include a policy of offensive aggrandizement. Quietism is self-immolation, a hatred of one's children and their descendants.

A hundred years ago Sandwich was called a dull and antiquated town, whose streets were narrow, dirty and unpaved. Now they are clean and neat and fascinating, and the town, with its three ancient churches and numerous other buildings of note, deserves a guidebook to itself. I find and enjoy, on my zigzag perambulations, no fewer than three secondhand bookshops – always the mark of an interesting town.

Bakers' shops and coffee houses are also irresistible, but I finally make an effort and begin my march to Dover, 15 miles south. From the quayside the way is through a children's playpark, then along a macadamized track between black fields. On an easterly course towards my old friend the sea, I am soon crossing the Royal St George's Golf Links on which a few people are having a game. Notices judiciously placed request the public kindly to keep to the footpath. It is well marked, signs at doubtful points indicating TO THE SEA, as if Xenophon might at any moment come by with his Ten Thousand, having taken a wrong turning somewhere in Anatolia.

The route leads through a pass between the dunes, and another notice says: BEWARE OF GOLFERS APPROACHING FROM THE LEFT. In the times of its greatness, any thieves caught in Sandwich were buried alive here, and it is eerie to be walking on them. Women thieves were taken to the river and drowned.

There is a slight breeze, and cloud is building up. If you are backpacking on such long-distance footpaths as the South Downs Way or the Pennine Way, there is the difficulty of obtaining and carrying water. The pathways go along the heights, away from streams and villages, and so to get water for the night's camp often means descending hundreds of feet. If you are not backpacking, you need to go miles off your route to find a hostel or guest house. The Saxon Shore Way, on the contrary, presents no such problem, since there are towns and villages all along it.

The dunes are covered in grass and other sorts of vegetation. If directional notices weren't visible, I would steer a compass course straight through, for the sea can hardly be missed. People push their electrically driven caddy-trollies around the course wearing funny hats. Golf became so popular that James II of Scotland decreed in 1457 that 'football and golf be utterly cried down and not used'. The game was introduced to Sandwich in the nineteenth century by a Scotsman, but goes back to Roman times.

Except for the footpath, the map shows a blank space. I reach the sea road at 11.07 and head south, the road quite busy with traffic.

Close to the beach the sea is light grey, but a black band 4 miles off shore   Royal St George's Golf Links

marks the line of the Goodwin Sands. There are lightships at either end and, when the sands are partly exposed at low water, many wrecks can sometimes be seen from Deal. The name had an ominous ring to any ship's captain, and still does. Some 50,000 lives have been lost, and shipping to the value of hundreds of millions during the last 500 years. It was long planned to build a lighthouse, but no proper support could be devised for its foundations. The sands were once the Island of Lomea, the last remains of which were carried away in the great flood of 1099. At low water the sands can be walked on, and cricket matches have been played there.

In 1703, during a four-day storm, thirteen warships were lost, and 1200 of their crews perished. A sailor of HMS *Shrewsbury* said how men 'climbed up the main mast, hundreds at a time crying out for help, and thinking to save their lives and in the twinkling of an eye, were drown'd. . . . I have not had my cloaths off, nor a wink of sleep these four nights, and have got my death with cold almost.'

The same storm damaged or wrecked 800 houses in London, and it was said that in Gloucestershire 15,000 sheep were driven into the Severn and drowned. The first Eddystone Lighthouse, with all its occupants, was swept away. In 1805 an old and totally unseaworthy troopship ran onto the Goodwins in thick fog, and 300 soldiers, as well as the crew, died with her. Even steamships tended to vanish too quickly for help to reach them on striking the Goodwins, many being lost on them during the First World War.

The sands also form a kind of breakwater, if you can interpose your ship quickly enough between them and the land. *Victory* spent three days in such shelter, known as The Downs, on her way home with Nelson's body from Trafalgar. Tradition says that the stone intended to build a sea wall was diverted by some greedy bishop to construct Tenterden church. Many wrecks have been entirely swallowed up in the sands. The banks are gradually moving landward and will one day, after our time, no doubt, join with the land.

Shingle between road and beach is easy on the feet. The tide is half out and people, as ever, potter about on the mud. Do any valuable objects break loose from the Goodwins and float on shore? If professional salvage experts dug deep in the sands they would no doubt have very good pickings.

Sea holly looks sturdy among sand, grass and gravel underfoot. A dark cloud ahead goes up to about 1500 feet, but has a silver lining. The road through the Sandwich Bay estate is private, though I suppose the RESIDENTS ONLY notice concerns cars, for there are bumps in the road to reduce their speed. A hovercraft comes towards the terminus at Pegwell Bay, with plenty of spray, and propellers in full spin. I once went to France in one, from necessity, but being cooped up as if in a smelly old bus was so unpleasant that I thereafter used ships which, though liable to pitch on a rough sea, and take longer, made the transit more civilized.

The hotel marked on the map – one no more – is a marine-looking building, white and grey. The cloud with a silver lining has gone, and others more nondescript have taken its place. From the Sandwich Bay Yacht Club there is a view back to the white cliffs of Thanet, with a few sailing boats on the darkening sea.

Walking by another golf course leads me to wonder whether this stretch can be designated the Golf Course Coast. The holes look like craters on a battlefield, and people walk between them with heads down as if they are searching for bodies that have not yet been collected after the fighting.

The track changes from shingle to stony, and patches of vegetation almost join to give a firmer tread. An enormous pile of driftwood is stacked on the beach, probably from ruined groynes, or beams detached from wrecks about the Goodwins. A group of buildings ahead never seems to get closer, and the pack of houses behind hardly appears to be farther away. Nor does the power station across the estuary.

Beyond Lydden Valley are low wooded hills. For twenty yards the track becomes wet sand, with horse dung and hoof marks. All too soon it is back to stones. Ideal weather for sailing boats outside the large breakers. Only a few arched foundations of Sandown Castle remain. It was built by Henry VIII at the same time as those of Deal and Walmer. Colonel Hutchinson (1615–54) of Nottingham Castle, and one of the judges of Charles I, was imprisoned here at the Restoration, and the place was so miserable (slightly more so for him than for his jailers, according to his wife's famous memoirs) that he died in six months and 'looked after he was dead as he used to do when best pleased with life'.

Much construction is going on along the sea wall. A small triangular sail seems like the outrider of a tanker coming up Channel. On Deal promenade, a squashed crab is colonized by bluebottles. Neat wooden groynes pencil down from the shingle.

I pass HM Coastguard at a quarter past twelve, Deal Rowing Club, a pub called the Forester, and an angling club followed by Deal Royal Exchange, then beach huts. The utility-looking pier is built on two piles and goes straight out to a ramshackle structure resembling a fort more than a pavilion of enjoyment.

On the front people sit in parked cars with beakers of tea and packets of lunch. Men smoke their pipes, safe from the wind outside. Last night I lodged in Deal, intending to walk along the front, but it rained so I went into Mister Brown's Restaurant, and the meal served by its lively waitresses kept me overlong. I also found the comforts of the Lynton Guest House too enticing.

Mrs Hutchinson, whose colonel-husband died in the castle, found Deal a 'cut-throat town', and she had good reason to; but thousands of sailors and ships' passengers owe their lives to the lifeboats of the Deal 'hovellers'. The men had, and still have, a reputation for daring and bravery, and no hoveller ever hesitated for a moment when a ship was in trouble on the sea.

'They cannot indeed be defended from the charge of certain malpractices with relation to wrecks; but these were exceptional,' says Montague

Dover Castle

Burrows in his book on the Cinque Ports (1888). 'And on the other hand their skill, intrepidity, generosity and contempt of danger have been the glory of sailor life.'

I call at a pub, shop for lunch, and continue south along the more dilapidated front towards Dover. The shingle is lined with fishing boats. Nets are hanging to dry, and some boats are under repair, or receiving that loving attention ever due to vessels with such names as *Mistral*, *Lady Frances*, *Gypsy Boy*, *Gypsy Queen*.

Elizabeth Carter, daughter of a learned cleric, was born at Deal in 1717. Her father taught her Latin, Greek and Hebrew, and she went on to learn French, Italian, Spanish, German, Portuguese and Arabic. She took an interest in astronomy, history and geography. She made the sum of £1000 from her translation of Epictetus, and died while on a visit to London at the age of eighty-nine. 'My old friend Mrs Carter,' Samuel Johnson said, 'could make a pudding as well as translate Epictetus from the Greek, and work a handkerchief as well as compose a poem.' To do him justice,

Crypt, Deal Castle

Johnson also told a famous Greek scholar that he 'understood Greek better than anyone I have ever known except Elizabeth Carter'.

The grand edifice of the Queen Hotel is derelict and being demolished – sky visible through the windows of its upper storeys.

Deal Castle is moated, circular, crenellated. Cannon at the walls were set to lob shot towards The Downs at any foreign enemy sneaking close. It was the most important fortress of the Deal, Sandown and Walmer line begun by Henry VIII in 1538 and finished in 1540. They were commanded by the Lord Warden of the Cinque Ports, but none served their purpose, due to the navy which kept all foes off. The only explosive to hit them was a German bomb in 1940, which demolished the captain's quarters of Deal Castle.

The paved way passes a placard saying that Julius Caesar landed on this foreshore on 25 August 55 BC. It seems a long time ago. Some of the boats lined up on Walmer strand have notices saying they can be hired by fishing parties, one proudly adding that an echo sounder is installed on board.

Walking needs fuel: I finish my sausage and eat rye bread and cheese. Along the beach, ramshackle boxes house the boatmen's tackle. Beyond the Downs Sailing Club I walk along a macadamized laneway free even of cyclists. Seaside houses of about 1880 line the road. A flurry of water indicates rain. It changes its mind, then comes on just as I am beginning to think it won't. Cumulus hangs over the Channel, but so high that no rain can last.

Walmer Castle, also moated and circular, has a battery of five cannon facing the sea, and six heavier guns on upper walls below the crenellations. Successive Lord Wardens have adapted the fortress into a dwelling house, and little of its military aspect remains, the cannon being mere decorations. Inside are relics of the Duke of Wellington: the camp chair he carried on his campaigns, his bedstead and the chair in which he died

Deal Castle

in 1852. The place is in good repair, apartments perfect for living in, windows clean and well aligned. Winston Churchill became Lord Warden in 1941.

Walmer Castle

Change maps onto the Dover Sheet of the new (1:25,000) Pathfinder Series, which are double the size of the older ones and have rights of way marked. Higher ground signifies the beginning of the cliffs. Between the macadam track and the sea, scrubland goes to meet shingle which shelves down to the water. The sea is choppy and dark blue under a range of stratocumulus.

The path, shingle and pools of water, goes along the backs of peculiar seascaped houses of about 1900. A line of beach huts and boats bring me to the Zetland Arms, in Kingsdown.

A narrow lane between the backs of houses takes me to a paved road, on a diversion from the private beach. Away from a steep wooded hill, and regaining the footpath, the sea is seen across two hundred yards of scrubland.

WARNING: WHEN RED FLAG OR LIGHT IS SHOWING THE RANGE IS CLOSED. There is no flag, so proceed – Sergeant Lamb. The South Goodwin lightship is 140 degrees magnetic. Pass the Royal Marines rifle range. Until recently 2500 Marines were stationed in Deal, where they had extensive parade and drill grounds, though the actual barracks were in Walmer. The corps was formed in 1664 as the Duke of York and Albany's Maritime Regiment of Foot, and battle honours were so many that their badge became a globe, to indicate they had fought in every part of the world.

WAR DEPARTMENT PROPERTY: KEEP OUT, so at a bend of the road I climb steps up the grey cliffs, a height marked on the map as Old Parkers Cap. At the summit I pass the only other hiker so far seen, a young man lying down with his backpack as a pillow, though he is curious enough to sit up and wave a greeting.

The view inland shows lots of houses, but many green areas also. To the north, beyond Pegwell Bay, the Isle of Thanet and North Foreland are visible. A few ships fade in the mist and distance, and the South Goodwin lightship marks the southern extremity of the sands. The cliff line of the coast of France is unmistakable. I pass another golf course, and the path goes through tall thistles, but is generally dry.

It is a pleasant meadow walk, one or two houses across the way, but otherwise no people. Inland are the Bottoms – East Bottom Farm, Otty Bottom and Otty Bottom Cottage, with Old Bottom Free Down beyond.

My pocket radio is tuned to 500 kilocycles and I listen to PCH from Holland sending instructions in Morse to ships. The path ascends, an easy walk, though the wind becomes colder, sky half cloudy with the occasional spray of rain. Grass grows right up to the edge of the cliff, a silhouette of waving stems with space beyond, nothing between it and the blue water. A slight depression of newly sown wheat rises up to the horizon, and in a dip is the solid clump of a dark green copse. The scene is entirely bucolic, apart from the golf course still seen on looking back.

On the roof of Leathercoat Point coastguard lookout a radar scanner goes round and round, the semicircle of a bull's horns continuously turning as if to charge anyone who might come in reach. It is almost as big as the roof to which it is attached. Perhaps the configuration of the land, just before reaching the war memorial, is conducive to increasing the velocity of the wind, because it comes strongly over the patch of black soil. The radar scanner completes a revolution every four seconds, so that even a rowing boat would find it difficult to get through the Channel without detection.

The memorial is erected to the Dover Patrol 1914–19: 'They died that we might live and may be worthy of their sacrifice.' On the base of the tall pointed pillar it says: 'To the memory of the officers and men of the Royal Navy and Merchant Navy who gave their lives in ships sailing upon the waters of the English Channel, 1939–1945.' The surrounding grass is neatly clipped, and there is an anchor at each point of the compass. On the east side it says that the monument was put up in 1921 'by public subscription together with those at Cap Blanc Nez, France, and New York Harbour, America. The names of those who gave their lives serving their King and country in the Dover Patrol are recorded in the Book of Remembrance in the Town Hall, Dover, a copy of which is kept in the parish church of St Margaret's at Cliffe.'

The stone was laid by Prince Arthur of Connaught, 19 November 1919, and the memorial unveiled by the Prince of Wales, 27 July 1921. I am awed at the thought of the numerous dead who went willingly to war, or were taken; or drifted in by circumstance, as are so many in war, and lost their lives after long accustoming themselves to danger, or so suddenly that little thought of the matter could be given. It was impossible not to salute all British seamen who had died around the coast of Kent, in acknowledgement of the fate that had taken them before their time.

On the descent to St Margaret's Bay, a notice says that the cliffs are dangerous if approached too close. Waves are heard breaking on the beach

The Winston Churchill Memorial Gardens, St Margaret's at Cliffe

as I go between trees and bushes. Cloud cover is complete. A flight of steps takes me by an old lookout point, and at three o'clock I am at sea level.

The only sign of habitation is the pub, which locks its doors the moment I get to it. If my curses take effect, the place will soon be a smouldering ruin. Twenty or thirty cars are parked, and a few people stroll by the water. Waves fall against the beach. There is nothing to stay for, so I walk along a rough and narrow path behind the pub, till I come to steps which lead back to the beach. It is confusing, trying to work my way out of the bay with the directions in the guidebook, so I snap it shut and, opening the map, immediately see what is wrong. I go up the road and turn left by the Winston Churchill Memorial Gardens, back to the cliff-top footpath, followed by the 'shrill-gorged lark'.

Patches of chalk show through the grass. Up ahead, rain clouds are forming, otherwise the dry wind is agreeable. To the right of a windmill, the latticework window of a lighthouse lifts above the trees. A Townsend Thoresen boat heads for Dover, and a Sealink ferry comes out. By the lighthouse, rain comes. In five minutes it stops, and at sea the perfect cone of rain is on its way in gusty wind towards Belgium.

Dover harbour is in clear plan below: quays, customs sheds, queues of cars and lines of lorries, warehouses and ticket offices. Better to be here with rucksack and field glasses rather than waiting down there to get on a boat. Gulls wheel along the cliff before flying side on to the ships – from where I'd seen their button eyes rove as they came in a perfect aerodynamic glide as if to move wings would reduce the acuity of their vision.

I semicircle the green depression of Langdon Hole. There are still a few miles. Beyond the town, Shakespeare Cliff is half obscured by rain and mist. One has to induce a kind of mindless plodding to put the miles

Old lighthouse and army buildings, St Margaret's Bay

Opposite Dover harbour east

Dover cliffs and harbour east

Opposite Dover cliffs east

Approaching Dover

behind and believe in progress. Hard to take note of every topographical feature.

The track divides, but which is the right one? I descend, keeping the course of an old railway line in view, still along the cliff but with its crestline to the right. Close to the harbour the track forks once more, the left heading for the bridge under the new road and down to sea level. It is a clear route, but on the map lacks the green imprimatur of a right of way. I see no difficulty, as long as it continues to exist. Near the bridge it narrows between clumps of bushes. The cliff has crumbled, a space too small for the feet to negotiate. It is perilous to go on, so I turn back and walk a mile, and join the proper track.

Two Dutch backpackers, set on the way for Sandwich, ask if there is a village in that direction. I assure them that they have only to keep walking, and after about 10 kilometres they will find one. They sound more cheerful at this information and head into the wind.

A walker thinks much of his belly, and I look forward to a good English tea in Dover. I want scones, bread and butter, jam, and an endless supply of tea. The path takes me under the brows of the massive castle and down to the sea front, among which houses Dickens placed Betsy Trotwood's chocolate-box domicile in *David Copperfield* at the end of *his* walk from London.

'The grating roar of pebbles' is drowned by traffic noise, and opposite Matthew Arnold's beach stands a line of hotels which look singularly averse to the afternoon tea business. A few minutes after half past four, I see a promising teapot palace in the main part of the town, however, and enter only to be told that: 'We've stopped serving.' So has every other place. I end up in a Wimburger joint where cups with tea in them are let out at 20 pence a time, and not sold outright by the quart pot, which is what I need in my dehydrated state.

The happy young waitress is amused at my request for a piece of apple pie and *two* cups of tea. Her lively eyes and curving lips show the curiosity of intelligence and the intelligence of curiosity. She wonders who I am – bearing a rucksack and wearing a beard, and wanting *two* cups of tea instead of one. Will one get cool while the other is being drunk? Or do I

want to pour it over my feet? And what will I do with the apple pie – for   Abbot's Cliff, Dover
which I refuse my allowance of whale-fat cream?

One cup goes down, and is immediately followed by the other, and she
sees this on turning with a sly glance from the rail twenty feet away. That
glance deepens her further. She gives it with an enhancing half-diffident
gesture, a mere quarter turn of the head that she thinks I won't notice. But
I do, and she responds to my smile; and when she comes over I ask for two
more cups of tea. She makes no comment, but her features are total
amusement held just below the threshold of an open smile. This is worth
all the walking alone out on the windy cliff tops, all the topographical
felicities of distant landscape. And the tea is good, even without sugar.

Such a smile in fact is worth all the cream-tea palaces in Cornwall.

Chapter Eight

Dover and Folkestone

Dover has always been an open door. The Germans had not been able to close it, nor the French and Spaniards before them, but it has taken many batterings.

The river which splits the town in two flows unnoticed, though in olden days it was wider at the mouth than now. *Dour*, and the name exactly denotes that which the place is not. There has always been too much coming and going for Dover to be anything but lively. Before Roman times all communication with Gaul led through. When the Romans attempted to land, the forts on either side of the harbour baffled them, and the great Caesar had to take his galleys and the men of two legions farther north to Deal.

Dover was never a natural port. There was trouble with silting, and still is, but it was closest to the Continent and easy to fortify. The land behind was open all the way to London, unlike ports on the Sussex coast which, having an impenetrable belt of forest spreading inland to the rear, prevented easy communication with the north.

Dover became the main Roman station on the Channel, the lynchpin between home and Albion, through which soldiers and administrators came and went. Two *pharos* or lights were erected on either cliff to guide ships from France – a perilous traverse in foul weather. But Watling Street began here, that straight road going to London and Wroxeter. Dover was the throat of the colony, and in the later Roman period became one of the great fortresses under the special control of the Count of the Saxon Shore.

Soldiers set the town on fire at the time of the Norman Conquest and were punished for it; but Dover had a unique place in the Domesday Book, commensurate with its significance to the nation in that it was the first place mentioned – though it was only the third in rank among the

Cinque Ports. Tradition says that the first castle was built by King Arthur, and in those days it was an awe-inspiring sight to any plenipotentiary – or would-be usurper. Hubert de Burgh held out in 1216 during the siege by Louis of France, thus saving England from a French dynasty.

The Maison Dieu of Hubert de Burgh gave hospitality to poor soldiers, often sick and destitute, coming back from foreign service. They were allowed to live there free for a fortnight. Multitudes of all nations and classes passed through Dover without let or hindrance from any immigration control. A charter of 1312 was especially based on the principles of fair play to the poor crossing the Channel.

Dover's greatest glory came when threatened by the Invincible Armada in 1588. Men and women lining the cliffs were filled with awe as 130 of the biggest and most heavily armed ships the world had yet seen sailed within range of Dover's fortifications, harried by the smaller ships of Drake, Hawkins and Frobisher. But the 150 English sloops and frigates were far faster. Dover roused itself for one last effort against the Armada: from then on the place went into comparative decline. It is nearly always so, that the great effort to save oneself is the one that finally kills, though it is not apparent at the time.

The ships of the English were feeble craft but, manned by expert sailors, they stung the Spanish fleet to death. Men of the Cinque Ports furnished 'the powder and match' for the fire ships which decoyed the great Spanish galleasses to their destruction off Calais. Every Cinque Port put in its quota of ships, men and expertise for this action which saved England from the evils of the Spanish Inquisition, just as the aerial battles over Kent in 1940 deterred the Germans from invasion and saved the country from barbarism.

The Dover Patrol during the First World War was a force of British and American naval ships, mostly destroyers, organized to protect military convoys and merchant vessels against German submarines and mines. In the Second World War the first big attack from the air came on 12 August 1940, and for much of the war Dover was bombarded by heavy guns from the French coast. The people lived in cliff caves for nearly four years, and most of the town was ruined. When I went there in March 1951 I wrote:

One would not think that the war had ended six years ago. These ruins look so established it's hard to imagine they were caused by war. Nearly all the hotels along the harbour front are empty and roofless, and behind their façades the extensive area of desolation is like the Cocteau Hades in the film *Orphée*.

There is no movement, only decaying walls and shuttered houses divided by narrow streets. Gutters are overgrown with dandelions, weeds crawl up blackened walls, and jagged rips shatter the vision. Pools of rainwater are trapped in uneven pavements. The cemetery in the middle is a grotesque collection of stones slanting irregularly to the sky, and all that remains of the nearby church is a gothic archway and a few windows in unsafe walls, through which small clouds cross the sky, a mobility that makes the empty houses seem more ruinous than ever.

The tarmac road at the seafront is rutted with disused tramlines. The sea comes up over grey shingle and flings itself against the wall. Gulls rise and fall on ridges and vales of green water, or curve and scream over the smashed houses, flattening before the wind like the German Stukas which did most of the damage ten years before. Past the breakwater and a moored trawler, the silver band of the horizon glitters in the morning sun.

Back in empty streets, doors have been ripped from shops and houses. Everything has settled down to orderly and inconspicuous decay. The framework of windows has fallen out, strips of wood in shreds. Wet wood hangs through a ragged hole that opens into the basement. Blue paper faded and rotten clings to walls streaked with damp. I look along their lines to the gaping hole where the stairfoot door should have been, then up to the bedroom from which the flight of stairs has disappeared.

Where there is no house at all, rectangular holes are like open tombs. Bushes with ten years' growth sprout their branches up basement walls and make tracks across the pavements. In one cellar the door has been ripped off, and blackened glass litters the steps.

A faded sign says TATTOO ARTIST A GREAT VARIETY OF DESI . . . . There is no silence while gulls screech across stratocumulus clouds, though finally they have no effect on such ruins. Black windows gape from taller buildings, and because of the silence, and there being no people, the area seems vaster than it is.

A black and white cat comes from a window, crosses the street and enters the doorway of another house. I hurry to the main street where there are shops and traffic, and where people seem unaware of the devastation.

Two hundred people were killed in air raids, and thirty by cross-Channel shelling. Seven hundred were wounded. A thousand buildings were demolished, 3000 seriously damaged, and a further 7000 received scars. Two thousand bombs hit the town, but shelling did the most damage.

*   *   *

The day is clear and cool, and there is a slight wind as I set out from the Priory station to do a further 15 miles. Dover Castle, starkly browed on the opposite cliff, never lets up its vigilance. Extended defence works dominate the wooded area below which stretches left and right above the houses of the town, its trees tinged with bright sunshine. Busy traffic to and from the port goes on twenty-four hours a day, and every day of the year.

Promenading Snargate Street, I pass the BRITISH SAILORS SOCIETY: SEAMAN'S RESIDENTIAL CLUB AND RESTAURANT, people inside having a snug and cosy breakfast. Shops sell boat equipment and fishing tackle, sextants, wind-speed indicators, compasses, and brass plates with such mottoes as 'The Captain's Word is Law', 'Dirty Old Men Need Love Too', and 'No Bloody Swearing' – to nail up on your boat and cause mild laughter.

This part of Dover, with its docks, newsagents, shipping offices and little hotels, is more interesting than the vast new hoverport. A radio shop sells transmitter–receiver rigs and CB radio gear. Radio has done much to make life safe and tolerable at sea. Even with a simple set, for direction finding and weather warnings – and a companionable voice – the sailor is conscious of never being entirely abandoned. Technology has so reduced the size of radios that even a long-range set can slide into a dufflecoat pocket. Heavier gear can include echometers, radar and wireless telegraphy. No wonder the industry thrives, and that Marconi is as worthy of canonization as Neptune himself.

Along Archcliffe Road the calm grey sea comes into view, a band of sunlight on it. South Military Road leads to Western Heights and HM Borstal in the Citadel, with its central chimney and single tower. A cul-de-sac is called Gloucester Way, it being no coincidence that Shakespeare Cliff, up a steep crescent, juts like an olive-grey chin into the sky.

A paved path parallels the road, green-painted railings flanking the beach twenty feet below. It looks as if it might be possible to reach Folkestone by going under the cliffs and following the railway, but my route lies along the top. It wouldn't do to be trapped by the tide.

A notice in a house near Sunny Corner says: BACK AT 9.30. Maybe the wife (or husband) has left for ever. A Ministry of Defence board warns that 'portions of this footpath passing through Lydden Spout Range Dover Area are closed during practice. On such occasions Red Flag warning signals are flown conspicuously near the Danger Area Boundary.'

Sounds of squealing and shouting come from a school. Allotment-garden cabbage leaves are riddled with holes. Halfway up the cliff the concrete path ends, and a look behind shows Dover harbour, as well as the castle, the borstal, the church on the cliffs, St Margaret's Bay in the distance, and two ships out at sea.

I look down from the very lip of Shakespeare Cliff. It is as impressive as Beachy Head. The wind is not enough to inch me towards the edge. Nor are falls of chalk sufficiently frequent or malicious to hit crows (which look much heavier than beetles) flying between the summit and the sea.

The first Kent coal was discovered near here, in 1882. Small chimneys ahead look like miniature martello towers, but are in fact air vents for underground caverns. To get the exact length of the railway tunnel that goes through the cliff is like trying to measure the distance in nautical miles between Cape Town and Kerguelen. Every attempt provides a different answer, though if one takes the average from the following guidebook figures it works out at 1366 yards, for what the fact is worth.

1417 yards – Black (1872)
1331 yards – Murray (1877)
1320 yards – *Highways and Byways in Kent* (1914)
1396 yards – Baedeker (1927)

Dover cliffs and Abbot's Cliff

New houses push into a re-entrant. The land rises towards a radio mast ahead. A boundary stone says: DOVER PEPPER MAYOR 1895–6. White cliffs are streaked with olive drab. Folkestone is already seen in the distance. Only 7 miles separate the two towns. White clouds are forming.

At the foot of Round Down I must be near Akers Steps, by which one may, albeit perilously, descend to sea level. A train comes out of the tunnel below. THESE STEPS ARE DANGEROUS. KEEP OFF. BY ORDER. BRITISH RAIL. The red notice has prominent white lettering. The well-defined footpath is marked by the acorn sign of the North Downs Way. A cleverly sited pillbox is set to take in flank a dip in the cliff, which would be the first point at which an enemy would appear after scaling it.

Between the foot of the cliff and the sea, mounds of British Rail material is spread over open land. Bands of sunlight give a stippled effect to the sea. A ship is coming into Folkestone. The visibility is not too good, because the French cliffs can't be seen. Four horses graze in a field, and sheep are dotted around. An old gun position sighted out to sea commands an expansive field of fire. The fixture for two guns is emplaced by concrete and steel girders.

Otter Cottage – or Peter Becker's Stairs – has probably long since been done away with to accommodate the railway workings. Otter Cottage was 'the Robinson Crusoe-like establishment of an old fisherman named Gatehouse, who with children and grandchildren pursued a variety of avocations, keeping goats, pigs and poultry, and looking out for flotsam and jetsam, and cultivating with success fig trees and vines against the lofty railway embankment,' according to Murray's guide of 1877. Probably the last happy Gatehouse left the locality when schools, taxes and census takers gleefully wiped out their Eden-like nest.

A distinct line of target butts appears on the horizon, without a red flag flying. There are no wild flowers hereabouts, only dull and withered grass. Cliff tops are deficient in flowers until yellow furze proliferates. A dump of plastic bags, tins, petrol cans, Coca-Cola empties, jam jars, bits of old radiator, bottles, the odd shoe, tiles and bricks are scattered at the cliff top. The path becomes a cart track, with eyes down to avoid the slop of soil and water which, at the next step, becomes mud, until coke and gravel is pounded hard to make sufficient stepping stones.

An alternative track of the North Downs Way is indicated for when red warnings flutter, but I can proceed by the normal route. Ventilation shafts, one of ten feet across, suggest many chambers housing military

headquarters and stores, and regional seats of violence for when the Bomb falls. Butts on the skyline are close enough to read their numbers. A fine view of Folkestone, and, far below, lines of surf come one behind the other across the beach of grey stones. The train goes under Abbot's Cliff. I look back at a fine sweep of the sandy-brown escarpment face, turning grey and white as it goes down to the beach, where a separate pool by the sea is distinctly enough shaped for use as a reference point on the map.

A large isolated concrete structure faces the sea, concave and rectangular, with a circle inside the rectangle. Neither notice nor indication is given as to what it can be. Such an ancient construction might seem plainly pagan, facing the sun and the sea and demanding sacrifices to justify the effort of building. But in fact it was said to be part of an early-warning system for Zeppelins in the Great War.

A concrete lookout point has a flagpole by its side, and a wire up the wood beats to the sound of the wind – clack, clack, clack – the two in concert with nothing but monotony to express, keeping the sombre beat going in case one day they will think of a significant message to tap out. The cart-track path goes parallel to the main road, with still a few miles before reaching Old Folkestone.

After Abbot's Cliff House at midday comes the inevitable caravan park, whose vehicles have an air of possessive permanency, mobile bungalows neatly parked, surrounded by flowers and clipped grass. The cliff is sheer, and close. Don't slip, I say. To allow that fatal step would not help in the laudable aim of wanting to live for ever. A train comes along the line like a child's toy set at Hamley's – minuscule and pretty. The railway threads a wooded area five hundred feet below. The toy train goes on working, with two trains passing. Fathers, bring your children here.

One or two yellow flowers of furze appear, by the noisy road and near the houses of Capel-le-Ferne. Groynes at the beach. A cross-Channel boat goes into harbour. There's some wind, but only two-tenths cloud, and the day stays fine. NO LITTER OR GARDEN RUBBISH. PENALTY ONE HUNDRED POUNDS – but quite a lot of money has been thrown away. Even the notice boards are litter.

Capel Court Country Club is a handsome white house. Folkestone in full view from the Eagle's Nest. At 12.30 I sit by the path and eat, an absolutely marvellous view over the Channel. A few patches of shadow, but otherwise the sun dominates the blue sea. Walk by the backs of bungalows, whose gardens are closely mowed lawns. The track is worn to a mini gully wide enough for one foot at a time to walk in, pointed dead

Martello tower, Folkestone

ahead and muddy at the bottom. Such a bicycle-tyre sort of track has been worn down by generations, so I walk by the side, where the grass is thick and deep, so that another track will soon be scored there.

A small tanker goes down Channel, and another ship from Folkestone ploughs to France. The rough path dips and narrows, with brambles reaching out, and a bushy part gets me back to the main cliff route. A young woman exercises three enormous black dogs.

Before the big descent by the Valiant Sailor, the whole of Folkestone is set out below, harbour, town and suburbs, going back into the country. Beyond, the coastline of Romney Marsh curves into the mist.

The descent goes over scabmarks of white where walkers have rubbed it bare of soil, but soon I am back on a concrete footpath and passing the first martello tower. The Warren is a rough patch near the town, but my way goes on to pavements. An alternative route leads inland via Caesar's camp, an equivalent distance to Sandling station, but I keep to the actual coast, preferring marine to bucolic scenery.

Two old ladies are at a bus stop: 'He didn't!' 'He did. And she did, too!' 'With a stick?' 'Well, I suppose you could call it that!' And the laughter came again, but I was soon out of ear's range.

Down steps to Folkestone harbour, by black rocks and then along Coronation Parade. A notice by a short cliff warns children against sliding, though many deep score marks show where they have done so. The Sunny Sands Self-Service Restaurant leads me to wonder whether the British are a nation of alliterates. I pass an amusement park with roundabouts, crazee golf, mini dodgems and other diversions. Pubs called the Bosun's Locker, the Ship Inn and Oddfellows Arms come up in rather close order. Ted's stall sells fresh jellied eels, whelks, prawns and mussels. After Dick's fish shop comes the Royal George, then Gigi's hot-dog stall, Manhattan amusement park and Rio's ice cream. I stayed in this port and seaside place in 1951, at Mrs Tryon's bed-and-breakfast boarding house.

The London and Paris Hotel has accommodation, bar snacks and coffee lounge. Lots of little boats in the inner harbour, with the usual anti-rabies exhortation: 'No dogs or other animals allowed in Harbour area.' A notice advertises day tours to the Continent: 'coach drive, meals, couriers to Boulogne, Bruges, Calais, Dunkirk, Ostend, Le Touquet'. An enormous anchor commemorates that 'The Sealink Car Ferry Terminal was opened on 3rd August 1972 by John Peyton M.P.'

The old-fashioned Royal Pavilion Hotel is being eaten into and demolished from the back. 'The Golden Mile of Amusements, with restaurants, markets and Rotunda Slippery Dip' – whatever that is, O Dreamland, I've come home!

A hydraulic funicular lift once took people to the upper part of Folkestone from the beach, but is now overgrown with weeds and bushes and will probably never be used again. At one time 400,000 people a year were carried up, and as many as 12,000 in a single day, at a fare of one new penny. Do people walk more nowadays, or drive around by car?

The hundred-foot cliff covered in greenery is in contrast to the grey sea. Dickens called Folkestone 'one of the prettiest watering-places on the south-east coast. The situation is delightful, the air is delicious, and the breezy hills and downs, carpeted with wild thyme and decorated with millions of wild flowers are, on the faith of a pedestrian, perfect.'

Modern Folkestone dates from the opening of the railway in 1844. A steamer service, started the year before, took four hours to cross to France. The crowds that once came here now pack the beaches of Majorca and Benidorm, though Folkestone has many visitors from Europe who

Opposite Folkestone harbour

want to escape the human pollution of their own watering places.

Eight-tenths cloud over a calm sea, with an enormous container ship halfway to the horizon, like three moving blocks of flats, suggesting a daylight flit in which you take your house with you.

Someone is calling Damon home. The mother shouts to his sister from the windshelter: 'Tell Damon to come!' – and Damon is nowhere to be seen. What's happened to poor Damon? The girl is plaintively calling his name. Did he drown, or was he kidnapped? Maybe he left home never to return, a departure planned to perfection for four of his eight years. He's out on the London road already. Mother joins the search. Damon is missing again. They look systematically, knowing his habits, until they find him giggling under a groyne. His mother sighs. His sister thumps him. They walk in silence to a car.

Seaside footpaths along the resorts are a constant mixture of movement, colour and distance. The walk is comfortable, no navigation problems, no mud, brambles or rocks to contend with.

Lees Cliff up in the town is prominent by its size and isolation. People on the roof look over the railings as if inspecting the place to buy it. It seems in fair condition. Some windows are curtained, others shuttered.

DO NOT DAMAGE OR REMOVE ROPE. A LIFEBUOY COULD SAVE A LIFE. IT MIGHT BE YOURS. Four tiers of beach huts are set back from the path. The container ship towing three blocks of flats at sea turns out to be Dungeness power station. The concrete way stops at a fence. After a patch of disagreeable shingle, the path appears again by some attractive villas. DANGER AT HIGH TIDE. Two middle-aged ladies talk animatedly, sitting in the sun. Part of the sea wall is cracking. Deep shingle over the path needs to be shovelled back. Built-up area near Sandgate, and I'm on the main road again. A grey-haired old lady in dark glasses, holding a handbag, walks by. She looks down, as if afraid of being old. Not at all. No one thinks they're old. I pass the Sandgate Hotel. Maybe she lives there.

Behind four martello towers lies Shorncliffe Camp. Barracks were first erected on the plateau in 1784. Its 200th anniversary is coming up. Sir John Moore trained some of the Peninsular regiments here, and Queen Victoria reviewed her troops before they set out for the Crimea in 1855. During the First World War the camp was the headquarters of the Canadian Army, and many Dominion soldiers are buried in the cemetery of the garrison church.

Cumulus clouds tower over the Channel and the bay ahead, though the

Sandgate

sky is blue inland. From the beginning of the Royal Military Canal, my bearing on the central tower of Dungeness power station is 218 magnetic.

A woman with a dog remarks: 'It's cooler now, isn't it?' It certainly is, and also an event to hear a few words. The peaceful footpath is muddy in places. The water reflects a white bird. Bushes come down to the opposite bank, and the faintest hum of traffic sounds in the distance. Trees are mirrored to their topmost roots, and bushes to the outermost twigs. A yellow triangular flag flutters on the golf course of the Hotel Imperial. The path is another dog walk.

Hythe means *haven*, and was a successor to one of the Roman fortresses placed under the control of the Count of the Saxon Shore. The High Street gives some variation of scenery and faces.

Ancient Hythe, with its steep streets, is another Dickensian maritime place, a superannuated Cinque Port with ragstone and weatherboard cottages. As one of the main Cinque Ports, Hythe had its tribulations, though in 1293 when French ships landed 200 soldiers, the townsmen, with sword and billhook, slew every one. A fire in the time of Richard II gutted the town. Five ships were lost and a hundred men drowned from the effects of an earthquake. When the River Leman silted up, trade and commerce diminished.

The Military School of Small Arms, founded at Hythe in 1854, became the chief school of musketry for the British Army, whose ranges are on the

Venetian fête, held every two years on the Royal Military Canal, Hythe

Hythe Bowls Club is one of the oldest in the country, founded before 1652

shingle banks west of the town. Sergeant Bostock gave instruction here, and in 1909 wrote his famous manual on judging distance. Thanks to such instructors, the British soldiers at Ypres in 1914 could fire their Short Lee-Enfield .303s with such rapidity and accuracy that the Germans wrote in their official dispatches that their attacks were held up by the British who had numerous machine guns, whereas they had no more than two to a battalion. Bostock was commissioned as lieutenant early in the war, but what his ultimate fate was I have no way of knowing.

I climb through the old town, a distinct smell of coal fires from the houses, to Saltwood Castle, a detour to see it if only from the outside. The place is strictly private and temporarily closed. Peacocks screech from the ruins. One can imagine the place under a full moon, with its moat, towers and circuitous walks from which to conjure up ghosts and phantoms.

The cock crows at Saltwood Castle, for it was here that the four assassins of Thomas à Becket rested on the evening before their dark deed in Canterbury. Two men landed near Dover, and two at Winchelsea, and the four reached Saltwood at the same hour. In the long winter night of 28 December, with candles extinguished, and not even seeing each other's faces, the plan was made.

From the muddy tree-lined bridle path I see as much as possible of the outside. A willow sleaves over the moat by one of the ruined walls. There is no way in. Let the eerie scene remain.

Hythe station, Romney, Hythe and Dymchurch Railway

On the way to Sandling station I reflect that England is jam-packed with 'desirable residences'. Every road, lane and field has its well-kept, well-gardened, well-watered and no doubt well-furnished house, with motorcars outside and all manner of gewgaws within. They gleam with prosperity and care, attractive with hung tiles or black and white beams criss-crossing in Elizabethan fashion (some of them genuine), or thatched roofs, or Sussex clapboard – or whatever it is. To my left, the playing fields; to my right, a school, with a warning advising motorists to go slow (they roar by like unheeding Spitfires) and to watch out for well-dressed children trying to cross. It's all very civilized, decent and almost reasonable, but how long, dear Lord, can it go on? Perhaps only the most wicked would not want it to continue for ever. Dells and meadows, fields and dingles, copses and woods and parks – everywhere to ramble and play, as long as you don't scare the pheasants, or shoo away the peacocks or poach the rabbits. A fat thrush looks at me, so fat it can hardly fly on such rich pickings. It is only the unemployed who might give trouble. But why can't they be resettled in Hythe, Folkestone, Sandwich, Margate, Ramsgate, Herne Bay? Billet them in the empty bed-and-breakfast places and allow them to walk along the beach and enjoy themselves, while those who can get on with the export trade and earn enough money from oil wells and overseas investments to support them.

I prolong my day's walk beyond Sandling station to Pent Farm, where Joseph Conrad lived. The house, behind corrugated farm buildings, doesn't look much of a place, though there is some resemblance to the photographs. A black dog in the garden wonders what I want. When Conrad had the house, there was probably space in front, but it looks very much of a working farm now.

I see the Old Man, with his sharp seaman's beard. He wears gaiters and leans on a stick, his eyes glinting for a change in the weather, or for disturbance from the fo'castle – but all the time thinking of Berdichev where he was born in 1857, seven years after Balzac was happy there.

Chapter Nine

Rain in the Woods

Ten-tenths cloud and a chill wind promises little as I set off on the penultimate slog from Sandling. At Slaybrook I turn right through a 'kissing gate' marked by a Saxon helmet to prove I'm on the right track. With a ploughed field on one side, and the dip of a stream on the other, the green path ascends gradually towards a line of woods.

Rooks fly over a spreading elm that bounces the hideous noises back at them. In the wood a muddy track goes between trees and bushes. Rifle noise comes from the ranges at Hythe. Ferns under the trees cover areas as large as fields. Passing an enormous oak tree surrounded by rose bay, I feel in my element, trekking through a forest by devious and muddy tracks, crossing Black Hill nearly 300 feet high.

Out in the open towards Pedlinge, winter wood is nicely chopped and stacked at the laneside. By Pedlinge chapel at half past ten I realize there's no avoiding mud today. Fifteen black bullocks follow me tamely to the fence.

The compass is my best friend. A very large ploughed field has no path: I don't want to disturb the clods of dark and dripping earth, nor be ankle deep in mud, so I steer a short course back to the road.

Shepway Cross is a mere junction: the earliest Courts of the Cinque Ports were held here in the open, before being moved to Romney. The Warden of the Ports took and received the oath on first entering on his office. Halfway down the leftward lane two boys are glassy-eyed as they puff up the hill on bikes. I turn right, go over a stile, and ascend a meadow towards a line of trees, hearing the noise of weekend flying from Ashford airport.

From the vantage point I see France under a thin dark line of cloud. Romney Marsh is below, a couple of martello towers at the Hythe end, and my eyes strain to pick out similar stumps along the coast.

Near Lympne a football match sways back and forth, twenty-two reds, blues and yellows bouncing between the goal posts. I head generally west, and from the trees glimpse Romney Marsh three hundred feet below. Visibility isn't good enough for it to be France I see far to the south. It must be a bank of cloud. I am eager to see the Continent because Albion's Little Island brings on twinges of claustrophobia. It is natural, going around the coast, that I should want to get out of it, and imagine every darker shade in the distance to be part of the mainland. The Romans looked that way to home and Rome, and the flaxen Saxons no doubt did so when they thought of better pickings elsewhere.

The cliff path goes along the ancient coast, the actual coastline being some miles south. On the road by the airport I keep the steep declivity to my right, sheep and cattle on its slope. The ruins of Lympne Castle are below, the Portus Lemanis of the Romans being their only harbour on Kent's southern face, the fourth of the Forts of the Saxon Shore. Towards the end of their power in Britain the Romans stationed a band of mercenaries here from Tournai in Belgium.

A parachutist comes down slowly over Ashford airport, though he is going to feel a bump, because all such landings are the equivalent of a jump from a twelve-foot wall. Eight goats chew in a field to my right. Farther along are geese. A man on a black and yellow hang glider goes up in a graceful curve from the airfield. I watch him detach the length of cable from the winch, and the second in which he turns in the air to get his bearings, and head hopefully into a thermal or wind, seems like an hour. The 300-foot drop-glide possible over the Lemanis escarpment is the most tempting direction, and he appears to swim towards it as if caught in some amniotic fluid of the sky. He floats in anticipation, then heads purposefully on a southeasterly vector. All seems well, till he suddenly goes round – with the alarming rapidity of a spinning top. I can hardly bear to look. All support gives way under him, and he comes down very quickly from several hundred feet, then vanishes behind a bank of trees. I imagine the worst, but hope for the best, and hurry on my way.

In the village of Lympne I stop by the churchyard to consult my map. A tall, burly, grey-bearded sexton comes out of the cemetery and asks if I'm lost. With a map in my hand I can never admit to being so, though he knows better and before I can say yes or no he points the way to the pub where, he says, I will find that the footpath I want continues out of the village.

I feel sure he was once a sailor.

A mile of main road is welcome because it means no mud, but in the region of the zoo park the directions specially written for the Saxon Shore Way indicate that I turn left and go down towards the Military Canal. A few caribou roam placidly around the field, as if half disappointed that predators can no longer keep them on the hop. They must be bored, with two-thirds of their faculties underemployed.

Somebody has been riding the track on a horse. A weird animal screams from its pen at the zoo park, causing me to reflect that I would not like to meet an escaped lion in this lonely place. I seem to have wandered into the safari zone itself, and suddenly there is a high fence blocking the track. I contemplate scaling it but, faint-hearted at the idea of meeting the inmates of the zoo park without a rifle, I retrace my steps back up the muddy hill.

Roman remains of Portus
Lemanis, now known as Stutfall
Castle

Lympne Zoo Park

I make several attempts to find a possible track to the Military Canal, but end up in jungle culs-de-sac or somebody's back garden, impossible to get out of without a kukri. A drizzle comes on just after midday, and I reflect that if a Roman had wanted to get from Gravesend to Rye he would have surely cheated on his time sheet and cut across country in about four days. He certainly would not have traversed each creek and climbed every hillock – or fiddled about on nonexistent footpaths – so that he took nine days on the matter.

By Brent House I try another likely looking footpath to reach the canal. After a fine field, a wood blocks the way, but I enter it and descend fifty feet or so, till I come up against barbed wire, which I climb over. I descend some more, then go under the next lot of wire and stamp down the third barrier. Still on the descent, I stumble against a fence of rotten wood to which a private property notice is attached.

Then I come to a more formidable barrier, and see a number of huts and wood stacks beyond. Short of having an armoured personnel carrier, or a few Bangalore torpedoes, or a sten gun with which to insist on a right of passage should my way be disputed by anyone emerging from the undergrowth, there is nothing to do but climb back up the hill, levering myself from branch to branch before finally reaching the road.

It stops raining at last. The proper itinerary of this part of the walk seems out of the question, and a pub on the road at Court-at-Street invites me in for a pint of the best bitter and a slab of veal and ham pie. Several men at the bar talk about the easiest or quickest or prettiest way to London by car, a discussion of such topographical complexity that, after they have politely ascertained from me, seeing my rucksack, where I am walking to and from where, they are still in the middle of it when I leave half an hour later.

From Postling Green little is visible except misty countryside and a black sea of newly turned earth. The church at Aldington was once the living of Erasmus, but he resigned within a year in exchange for a pension of £20. Another local celebrity was Elizabeth Barton, 'the holy nun of Kent', who in her epileptic fits – on one occasion attended by priests, clerics, and three thousand of the 'common people' – prophesied among other things that if Henry VIII divorced Queen Catherine he would not reign another month. Epileptic or not, such slipshod utterances caused both her and her patrons to be executed by the enraged Henry at Tyburn in 1535.

There are poppies and daisies in a cabbage field. Someone behind a

Aldington Knoll

Opposite Chapel of Our Lady, Court-at-Street, with army pillbox attached

garden wall at Copperhurst is burning vegetation, smoke clouding the road. A footpath between cottage backs brings me once more into enormous fields of black loam, broken ridges shining with wetness where the blade has cut them smooth. Through drizzle and mist I get into a field of sheep, and head towards power transmission lines, the pylons going parallel to the footpath. There is no mistaking the rain. I maintain direction by keeping the snug-looking residence of Cobbs Hall well to my right up the hillslope.

My course descends through a meadow, then goes between two fences and into a wood. The pylons are my guide, because path markings do not exist. Once in the wood, the power lines above the vegetation are always there, and as long as I keep them in view I can't go off track. It's impossible to take a compass bearing, even supposing I could see any identifiable point, for with such power lines so close the needle spins as crazily as a raindrop in a gale.

Near Aldington

Getting through bushes and high grass is difficult. Branches and leaves empty rain on to me in sufficient quantities to turn my Grenfell jacket black. The brambles and high grass, while soaking my trousers, are at least useful in scraping the mud lumps from my boots. Plates of rain bomb down from the tree tops. There is no track through the dense undergrowth, though I am obviously following close to and in the general direction of a watercourse. In a wood you always reach water sooner or later, even if all but invisible under its mat cover of foliage. Keeping the pylons in view, I must some time come to a gravel road, but the rate I move through thicket and bramble means it will be later rather than sooner.

Seeing daylight to the right, I decide to get out of the wood and walk along the edge. Looking at the map, still dry in its covering, and taking off my bespattered glasses to do so, and rubbing water from the plastic case with a wet finger – which action tends only to displace the liquid domes – I see that, even at this comfortable scale, the multiplicity of hair lines is confusing.

The footpath doesn't go through the wood at all, but along the edge, in which direction lies the daylight just seen. Apart from the dotted indication of the footpath, there is a pecked line joining the pylons, plus the faint score of the wood's marked limit, as well as the blue indication of the stream, and an orange contour line, thus making five marks crossing and recrossing within a couple of millimetres, distorted by rain on the plastic which covers the paper.

Voices sound from the outside. Am I trespassing on a gamekeeper's preserves, and ruining his pheasant-breeding programme for the next five years? Two men are obviously searching for something, or someone. In my green jacket I am invisible, even to the trained eye of a gamekeeper, but only as long as I don't move. Perhaps they have already heard me crashing through the undergrowth like a bull elephant on its way to the psychiatrist. However it is, I am in no mood to conceal myself, and in any case have no reason to.

A breakout is the only course, but it is going to be difficult to get through fifty yards of close bushes, cross a stream and deal with a fence. I ask in a loud voice if they happen to be on a footpath, and one of them answers that they are. Forcing a way through, I set myself to get over the stream. Stepping on layers of brambles and ferns, which hold me above the spate of water, I reach for one branch, and then another that looks strong enough, till I can lever myself forward and leap onto more solid earth.

The fence is easy after this and, once clear, I see the two men who, still looking anxiously over the fields or into the wood from which I have emerged, ask if I have seen a flight of ATC cadets during my walk. They have lost twenty boys who set out on a cross-country walk to do 10 miles today and 5 tomorrow. I suppose the two men, probably their officers, have to guide them and check their progress over certain parts of the course.

If the cadets have any sense, I intimate in my cold and saturated state – and I once had four years as an ATC cadet in which to discover that at such an age one has a great deal of sense – they are holed up in a steamy café with mugs of tea and wads of cake while waiting for a bus to take them somewhere even cosier for a night stop.

Near Priory Wood, Bilsington

Again wiping water from the map, I show the officers the route I have taken, and say I saw nothing of their boys. They have a van on the nearby road, and set off to search the environs of another likely crossing point.

I am glad to be out of the wood and on tarred lanes for a while. A

detention centre near Easton's Corner seems as dead as if the inmates have absconded en masse for the weekend. The path goes by Hungry Hall, which name inspires me to crouch by a hedge and, despite the pouring rain, consume some food and hot tea.

Such weather depopulates the countryside. I see no one. It wouldn't be difficult to make a clandestine way across this kind of wooded terrain, though with somewhat more care if one were actively searched for, especially around paved roads and through clearings.

I enter more forest on my way to St Augustine's Priory. I want to light my pipe, but the matches are wet. A ploughed area shows no evidence of the footpath. From where I stand the field looks like a sea of petrified black wave crests, and I am reluctant to steer myself across. Apart from fearing to sink into the mud, or be jacked two feet higher by it and end with much weightier boots, such an operation is navigationally tricky. It is equally so to go around by the hedges, because changing direction three times, when the sides of the rectangle are not always straight, though they may well appear so, invariably gets me back to the wrong point, and not at the entrance to the next wood. Whatever method used, one has to pick up the footpath where it carries on from the mire of the field.

In going around a field, therefore, the errors can accumulate instead of, as in certain kinds of navigation, tending to cancel each other out. I use my binoculars so as to have a positively identifiable point at which to arrive, in this case a conspicuous tree. Another problem in going around the edge of a field is that the parsimonious ploughing has in fact left hardly any grass to walk on. You either go too far into the hedge to avoid the mire, and get twice as wet from water-laden branches, or stumble over the mud you had taken such trouble to avoid. Going by the hedges also trebles the distance, but I decide to try it.

I walk quickly, the rain giving no incentive to linger. Tough brambles grow sneakily out from the hedge bottom, and on one of these I trip. There is a slow-motion sprawl into the mud. I curse the joys of nature as the unlit pipe flips from my mouth, and both arms go forward to take the weight. A hundred yards farther on, the spectacle repeats itself. Who would be out on such a day?

I find the entrance back into the wood by the right footpath, but then wander two hundred yards off course, for when I come out from the trees and get over a fence, I find myself in the private grounds of the Augustinian priory. Little survives from its foundation date of 1253, but it looks romantically impressive in the rain.

Sounds of cheerful revelling come from the refectory as I walk through the main gate to the road. A few hundred yards south I enter Priory Wood, seeming to have lost the course, but made a good track.

Moss and mud are churned up together. The wood is sparsely treed, but a large red circle is painted on the occasional trunk to indicate the way. In dry weather the route would be paradise, but today it is a long yellow quagmire mulched with leaves. Potholes are full of water as rain comes down. Otherwise it's beautiful. I'm wet but not hungry, and manage to light my pipe on striking a match against the underside of a piece of dry branch.

In the next wood the rain is less intense, though the mud is the same. An airliner flies above the weather. At another large ploughed field of black loam-waves I steer a compass course straight across, missing the entrance to the wood by only five yards, so that I have no trouble spotting it.

The wood is full of dead pine trees twenty feet tall, one or two green bushes feebly growing between. The sere effect is only alleviated by a scattering of toadstools under the occasional birch tree. I walk along with no complaints, smoking my pipe, almost accustomed to the vile weather.

The red circles painted on the trees diminish in frequency till they disappear altogether, but not before tempting me so much off course that I miss the path and keep going on a more open ride which comes to a dead end. I feel like a fly caught in the bottom bulb of an eggtimer. I barge to the edge of the wood, and a bearing on Stonegate Farm tells me where I am. Back on track, the last part of the lane is particularly muddy, and a log trips me flat into the mire.

I begin to think that this section of the walk should not be considered part of the Saxon Shore Way. Swimming in the sea would be easier, and there'd be no mud. No Saxon or Roman – nor even a benighted Briton – would be seen dead on this route, though it is undoubtedly a marvellous exercise in cross-country orienteering. A part-time member of the army would be in seventh heaven. The only advantage for myself is the indication that I must be fairly fit to be able to do it.

At four o'clock, by Horton Farm, I've never been in such a quagmire. South of Gill Farm it gets worse. I sink two feet into it. I walk to the left of the path, which is slightly better because a few logs have been put down, probably by someone who was at Passchendaele in the First World War. Ingenuity fails and I leave off the effort of zigzags and splash openly through.

In the nature reserve the track improves slightly. It isn't raining any

Priory Wood

more, though that's only a comparative assessment. The potholes made by horses' hooves are full of yellow water. Getting to the edge of the path to avoid the deepest part of the slosh means being tripped by more ubiquitous brambles which have grown out from the shrubbery.

A man of rough appearance and about forty years of age suddenly appears from the bushes. He is wearing peculiar Oxfam kind of clothing, and has an open umbrella. He asks if he can have some of whatever is in my flask. Whether from privation or lack of use, or whether it is congenital, he can hardly talk. The flat cap he wears has no crown, and the black hair that shows through falls unevenly as if he clips it himself. Or perhaps he lives with a soulmate in his remote shelter of leaves and branches, which must be a good one because his clothes are as dry as summer wheat.

A long beard is tucked like a scarf into an ancient waistcoat which he has taken great care to preserve in one piece. It is this garment which tells me he may have seen better days, for it is held together over his chest with a large pearl button top and bottom, and bits of string which haven't been undone since, in a moment of inspiration, he threaded them there.

I give him the rest of my tea, and a cheese sandwich. We stand, his brown eyes bent to the food which he fastidiously chews. When he finishes I offer the £1's worth of coinage in my pocket, but he grunts and shakes his head, which puzzles me for I want to do something.

He reads me well, and holds his middle finger to a sapling, making a sawing motion. Something to cut with. I feel in my pack for the sturdy black penknife, knowing I have another at home. His hand shakes as he grasps it. The hand opens slowly, and he stares as if afraid to unfold the blades in case the knife should turn out to be made of shadow. He thanks me distinctly, and goes back into a thicker part of the wood. Then I wonder how many such knives he has in his sylvan hideaway.

I catch the shriek of a diesel train on its way to Ashford. The man of the woods must often hear its noise, and decide to keep far from its track. But never was there a sweeter sound to me. Even only a few hundred yards away, I am still up to my ankles and at times knees in the ooze. There's nothing to do but splash on to the end.

The sound of an ice-cream jingle comes on the wind from the village. At half past four I get out of the nature reserve. A few minutes later, thanking God for the invention of the compass, I cross a field and hit the railway station right on the nose, following signs to the ticket office.

Chapter Ten
The Military Ditch

The first day was long, and the last will be short. Perhaps the Saxon Shore Way ought to be done in reverse, beginning with an amiable amble from Rye and working up to the long marches that come later. However that may be, I stride out of Ham Street station on a cloudy morning and go down by handsome Home Farm to turn right at the Duke's Head. The Old (unmistakable) Iron Duke looks icy as ever from that pub sign, eager for the first sight of You-know-who coming across the Military Canal.

Much traffic passes between Dungeness and London, and east and west between Kentish ports and the back end of Sussex, but the village of Ham Street is hardly mentioned in the guidebooks – and in some not at all. The railway station, however, was used at one time by Henry James who lived in Rye, as well as by Joseph Conrad, Ford Madox Ford and Stephen Crane. Little more than a crossroads, there is not even a church, but with shops and a pub it makes a convenient staging post on the Saxon Shore Way.

Queen Anne's lace by the roadside is brown and sere, as if abdicating after the long Marlborough summer. I turn right and go under the railway bridge, the cross-country footpath starting at a stile by Viaduct Cottages, where serious navigation begins. I steer across the fields and keep Warehorne church as far as possible in the one o'clock direction – as we used to say on the firing ranges.

The track at first confuses, then becomes more distinct, and even mysteriously macadamized in places. I observe an adolescent rabbit. It has seen me and can't move, so I clap my hands and watch it run for the safety of a hedge. The railway to my left and the church tower ahead are good landmarks, and soon lead me to the village with its pub and shops.

Once the scene of an important fair, Warehorne is no more than a cluster of pleasant houses surrounding the green. In 1871 the population

Warehorne church

was 507, but now it is only 290. The austere church is nevertheless well lit, with pews like deep boxes which cut people off from each other while at their prayers. The tower was damaged by lightning in 1777, and rebuilt in brick.

Through the cemetery and into the fields, a bit of map-and-compass work is needed to get me to the Military Canal. I walk quite close to cows and their calves, but none of them move. The cows are exhausted from having given birth, and the calves are still too stunned to stand up and see what the world is all about. Perhaps they have already been told it is only grass. They lie all over the place as if dead, and it's like walking through another kind of cemetery.

There's no way through the fence, so it's over the barbed wire, my rucksack going first, then me following. The matter is accomplished without a tear on my trousers, and then I leap a ditch to get onto the bank of the Military Canal. With green pack, green trousers and Grenfell jacket, nobody can see me and complain that I am despoiling their boundaries. Only a flash of the map might give me away, and those provided by our considerate Ordnance Survey are now between green covers. Childhood habits of melting unseen into the countryside die hard. I get up onto the canal bank and look across at the expanse of Romney Marsh to the south.

The Royal Military Canal, which runs from Hythe to a point near the Isle of Oxney, where it joins the canalized River Rother, is about 23 miles long and was excavated in 1805–7 during the Napoleonic invasion scare. Along the coast itself dozens of martello towers were built, so called after Cape Mortella in Corsica where a round tower of the same type had proved so difficult to capture by British troops in 1794.

Sixty feet wide and eighteen feet deep, the Military Canal was intended for defence, but also served for the conveyance of stores and troops, a lateral feeder for the firing line. For some years afterwards a steamboat ran along its course, and during much of the nineteenth century it was still used for the transport of road material. Small houses erected at mile-long intervals for use as signal points, or for artillery-observing officers, were later lived in by pensioners of the Ordnance Department, who acted as 'walksmen' and supervised the traffic. In the beginning the bank was raised to protect skirmishers, and military stations, at one time occupied by coastguards, were placed along its length.

At every angle of the bank, embrasures for cannon were constructed, ready in case Napoleon's army, assembled in the camp of Boulogne, should descend on the coast. He finally lost his appetite for the adventure because of the unbridgeable Channel and the undefeated Royal Navy.

The water barrier of the canal was again prepared for defence in 1940. Concrete pillboxes were sited along the northern bank, and though it would not have held back a concentrated attack by armoured forces, it might have served as an anti-tank ditch for a few vital hours. The first pillbox I came to after leaving Warehorne had a good field of fire, commanding the nearby bridge of the Ashford–Hastings railway.

A walk around an island coast must obviously deal with fortifications, but a reading of Napoleon's military maxims indicates that he might not have landed on the south coast at all, being aware of what preparations were being made to prevent him: 'A well-established rule of war is not to do anything which your enemy expects of you – for the simple reason that that's what he wants.' Perhaps he would have descended on the north bank of the Thames, opposite those forts referred to at the beginning of this walk, and there fought the great battle before marching on London.

The Military Canal was a ditch rather than a river, and even rivers ranked only third place as obstacles to an army in Napoleon's view. But whatever effect the canal might have had, it is now an area of great natural beauty. Most of the elms are gone, but others, tiny in their protective boxes, have been planted along the bank.

Beyond another pillbox, offshoots of water are occupied by two handsome swans. The red-tiled tower of Kenardington church provides a convenient landmark. A fisherman on the other bank waves a greeting. Sheep graze on the flat marsh side, and cattle browse on higher ground to

Pillbox, Royal Military Canal

the north. I enter a field of young bullocks and, when one won't move out of the way, tap it on the nose so that it does.

A white handkerchief lies on the path, as if signalling the spot for a helicopter to land. Trees along the ditch sigh in the wind. The fitful sun comes and goes. A pillbox before the Kenardington bridge reminds me that in the ninth and tenth centuries the people of that village constructed earthworks here, at that time on the coast, to keep off harrying seamen.

The view over the canal is obstructed by bushes and small trees. The higher of the two paths is more difficult, due to nettles and brambles, but favoured because of possible views. Every walker must do his bit to keep the way open, but I tire of crushing thistles and change to the lower and wider path. A high-winged single-engined monoplane with fixed undercarriage passes overhead, going northwest, flying perhaps from Lydd to Lashenden near Headcorn.

The bucolic way at times seems dull. I miss the sea, or a touch of interesting squalor. Pylons, never far away, follow the canal. A train comes out of Appledore station. There are many dragonflies, nature's helicopters performing incredible aerobatics. Gulls sweep and squawk along the canal, as if in their ancient memories believing that the high land behind is still the real coast. Or maybe they are feasting on succulent dragonflies that venture too high.

Three youths are fishing on the opposite bank, and one calls to another, in rough but impeccable rhyme: 'Oy, Roy!' – for which he gets a very obscene response. A couple and their three children walk by with blankets and picnic boxes. The adults avert their ears at the youth's swearing, but the children are delighted.

The noise of machinery comes from Appledore's Answer, the largest bulb farm outside Holland. BULBS FLOWERS POTATOES says a notice at the entrance. In the flowering season the colours of red and yellow can be seen from such a distance that private fliers use them as a landmark.

The village has a baker's shop and smithy. The Red Lion looks very welcoming, with tables outside. A man of about seventy at the bar notices my map, and says he was in this area during the war, when the locals, he tells me with a mischievous false-teeth smile, were rushing about with popguns and pitchforks waiting for the Germans. He is on holiday, and lives in Reading where, he says, he has a briefcase full of army maps from 1940, when he was in the Royal Engineers. He did a lot of walking himself, as well as cycling, but now that the demon rheumatism has taken over he is too old for it. He swigs what looks and smells like half a pint of neat

Near Appledore

whisky: 'The only thing that keeps it off,' he grins. 'Some of the time, anyway,' he adds when a twinge gets him. Over my second drink in the doorway I watch him drive off on a large motorbike.

Appledore has always been a front-line town, either from the sea or foreign enemies, or both. The town raised here by the Saxons (it means apple tree in their language) stood on the bank of the then tidal Rother. The Danes demolished the place in 893 when they sailed up channel in 250 galleys. After being burned down by the French in 1380, Appledore seems to have had no disaster since.

Across the road from the pub is a rusty artillery piece which looks as if it has been dug out of the marsh, something like an old 25-pounder, which its owner might one day lovingly restore should an enemy threaten to come north again over the nearby bridge.

The way inland passes a house called The Quillet, and then The Quillet's Garth, before going over a stile into open country. From an eminence can be seen higher land some distance away, known as the Isle of

Oxney, a few square miles and two villages once surrounded by water.   Oasthouse near Appledore

Sheep scatter as I walk towards poppies, daisies and agrimony on the marsh. One sheep runs and the others follow. Deep ditches seem cut at random, so it is essential to keep to the route and find footbridges to get across. The footpath is unmarked so I bring out the compass and head for the Ferry Inn.

A mass of sheep swirl and bleat in the next field, where a man is training a sheepdog, for he snarls: 'Lie down, you mongrel!' The poor animal flattens, wants to be trained, but instinct gets in the way. He trembles, craving to be up and harrying the sheep. The fierce cry comes again: 'Keep still, you — brute!'

The tail flicks, the nose lifts. Unable to please, he longs for a signal. The man walks, and the sheep disperse. Even to make a mistake is more tolerable than hugging the grass. The man grumbles, then gives a signal. The dog circles, gathers the sheep into an invisible noose, and belly along

Reading Sewer

the ground, intimidates them towards a gate.

Corn is cut, and I have to tread over it to reach the bridge. When Oxney was an island the ferry was here, and a list of prices is marked on the inn wall. Only dogs, it was said, were let in and out free. The marshes around Oxney have long since been drained, and roads cross it from all points, so that a motorist in a hurry might not even suspect its existence.

Foregoing the saloon bar, I follow a cart track by a canal called Reading Sewer, which is almost as wide as the Military Canal. Swans lord on it, and yellow waterlilies proliferate. A kind of celandine with five bright petals grows among scores of green lily pads so close they look like the outer tiles of some fairy dwelling place.

The pale and gentle mount of Chapel Bank is west-northwest, over seventy feet above the marsh. Clumps of trees grow at its summit. There are ruins of an ancient church on what was once also an island, but walkers need good boots against adders which regard the place as their own.

Stone Cliff and nearby farm

A concrete lane runs close to it, but I turn south to pass Luckhurst Farm and make my way around an unharvested potato field, before crossing more fields to the Crown, Stone's other pub. Stone was destroyed by Danish pirates in 991, and I imagine the villages along the old sea coast were not unhappy after the great storms of the thirteenth century had caused the sea to retreat and leave them in peace. The nearby club hut of the British Legion is lettered dazzlingly clear, impossible to miss: 1914–1918 MEMORIAL HALL.

The embowered lane ascends towards the church, cool from the sun, hidden from the wind. There is a Roman altar to Mithras in the church, on which the relief of a bull can still be seen, said to have been used for blood sacrifices. How it survived in a Christian edifice is anyone's guess, though the Reverend William Gostling, who was vicar in 1753, had it thrown into the garden, where it lay until the early years of this century.

The uphill road puts a strain back into the legs. Three house martins rest on a telephone wire. When I look again there are five, evenly spaced,

View over Rother Levels and Walland Marsh

Opposite Rye harbour

then six, and finally seven, a row of beautiful unmoving birds with the vibrations of telephone speech going through their feet.

The walk leads across fields and between two farms to the eastern back of Oxney, the path invisible until it begins to descend the two hundred feet down Stone Cliff – from which one can see far over the Rother Levels and Walland Marsh. But nothing is distinct because the day is hot and columns of smoke rise from burning fields as if one is approaching the extensive front line of some bitter battle.

Not only have the Danes landed in this fair and fertile region, but it is as if every other enemy – not least the French and the Germans, as well as the Spaniards – have joined forces to loot and burn. The sun is unwilling to break through such palls of funereal smoke and reveal the distress of its inhabitants.

The descent of Stone Cliff is almost alpine in its steepness. Once down, I lose my way among the maze of ditches that cut up the wheat and potato fields, but eventually reach the road at the boundary stone dividing Kent and Sussex.

Getting through a fence takes me back onto the high bank of the Military Canal. Small boats are moored by the score from Iden Lock, where the canal joins the tidal River Rother. Here I cross onto the marsh side, and as the day goes on draw more into myself, not looking back and paying little notice to whatever hovers in the distance. The feet automatically take me forward, the knees lifting to climb a stile, and I go on through fields speckled with sheep and cows. The lumpy path always looks smoother on the other side of the river.

A man crossing Boonshill Bridge in a Mercedes car seems curious about me, and in a friendly fashion winds down his window to remark on the fine day. We discuss the natural history of the canal, and agree it is more beautiful and interesting in the other direction than the one I am walking in. He asks if I want a lift into Rye, the first time on the walk that anyone has made such an offer.

The tide is out, leaving a trickle between low mud banks. The crew of a boat wave to me, an eccentric walker only one rung down the evolutionary scale to those who mess about in boats. Their well-loved vessel seems becalmed, as if they daren't move for fear of getting stuck, for the narrow channel is almost devoid of water.

Rye

The triangulation tower of Rye church is 3 miles away. The Ypres Tower is also visible which, because of the First World War, became the *Wipers* Tower, after the infamous salient in Belgium. I stand having a piss, my back to the canal and the road, and the sheep walk away in disgust at such unseemly behaviour.

There is the smell of seaweed, rank water and salty air. The usual tideline rubbish comes almost to the grass: a plastic bag, a hand towel, a rubber glove, a few bottles and bits of wood. There is also a single enormous rubber wader, as if a one-legged fisherman had gallantly sacrificed his life to rescue someone who had no legs at all.

Under the railway bridge, stepping stones across the mud are firm enough to support my weight. The day is dry and hot. By back gardens I reach the A259 and turn right towards Rye, the goal of my long trek by riverbank and seashore, cliff and estuary, field and canal, marsh and midden, and a linseed layer cake of smells around the coast of Kent and into Sussex, a 140-odd miles punctuated by forts and burial mounds, jetties, villages, woods, caravan parks, wharves, creeks, pubs, docks, factories, power stations, holiday resorts, as well as farms, orchards and sheepfolds, giving as much variety as any walker could wish for.

I go into Rye through the ancient Landgate erected in 1360, the survivor of three which once guarded the town. The leftward view over marsh and meadowland shows Rye Harbour and the winding Rother going to the sea.

Every street in Rye is of interest, cobblestoned ways winding up and around and through the town. Some of the houses would no doubt have been even older if the place had not been burned and pillaged so often by the French in the fourteenth and fifteenth centuries. When the sea was below its gates it was a frequent point of departure for the Continent. Such prosperity made it a standing temptation to be sacked.

The sea began to recede from 1600, though even as late as Charles II's day a 50-gun battleship could safely navigate the harbour stream. Much importing and exporting of goods still takes place, and dozens of small boats have their moorings here. It is a sailors' town, and retains a curious Flemish atmosphere.

Henry James lived in Lamb House from 1896 until his death in 1917, where one can see mementoes of his life and work. The summerhouse in the garden, in which he wrote his novels, is no longer there. The only German bomb which fell on Rye during the war, with unerring Teutonic instinct, blew it to pieces.

I turn up East Street and pass the Flushing Inn till I come to the church which has been called 'The Cathedral of East Sussex'. There are some fine oil paintings and much stained glass inside. The building did not escape being set ablaze by the French in 1448. But all that has changed now, I hope, as I go down the hill to get the bus to Wittersham, the nearby village on the Isle of Oxney where I live.

Henry James's garden, Lamb House, Rye
(in the care of the National Trust)

Maps

The diagrammatic maps which follow the general map of the area are reproduced by kind permission of Dr Andrew Gray and the Kent Rights of Way Council from their pamphlet guide, *The Saxon Shore Way*.

Readers wishing to walk the route followed by Fay Godwin and Alan Sillitoe, including their occasional deviations from the officially designated footpath, may find it advisable to acquire, in addition, Ordnance Survey maps, 'Landranger' series, nos. 178, 179 and 189.

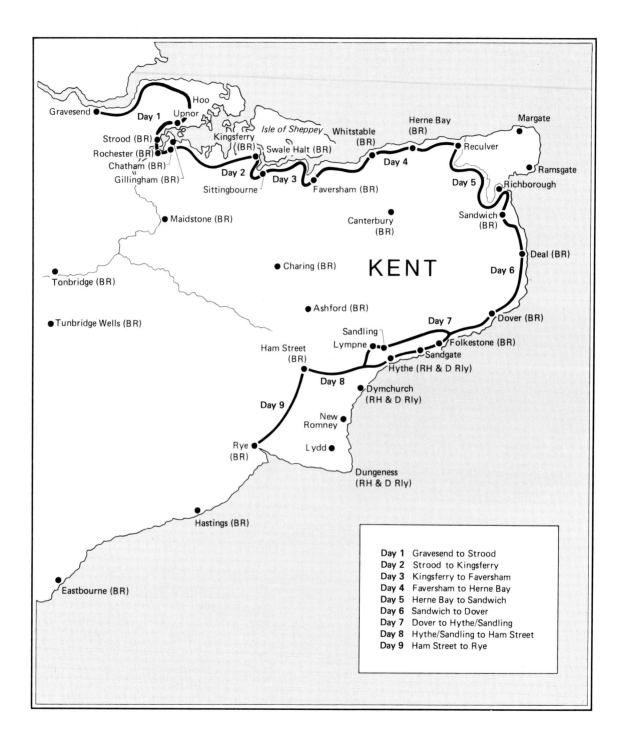

Day 1 Gravesend to Strood
Day 2 Strood to Kingsferry
Day 3 Kingsferry to Faversham
Day 4 Faversham to Herne Bay
Day 5 Herne Bay to Sandwich
Day 6 Sandwich to Dover
Day 7 Dover to Hythe/Sandling
Day 8 Hythe/Sandling to Ham Street
Day 9 Ham Street to Rye

iles)

?r-Roc	32.1	KLS
	20	MIL
?c-SW	35.8	KLS
	22	MIL
N-Fav	33	KLS
	20	MIL
?-HB	23.5	KLS
	15	MIL
B-SAN	31	KLS
	20	MLS
?N-DOV	25	KLS
	15	MLS
OU-ETCH	21	KLS
	13	MLS
TCH-HAM	24.5	
	15	MLS
HAM-RYE	22	KLS
	14	MLS
YE-HAS	20	KLS
	13	MLS

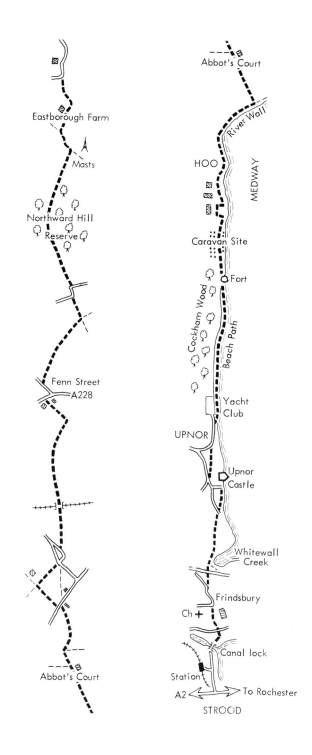

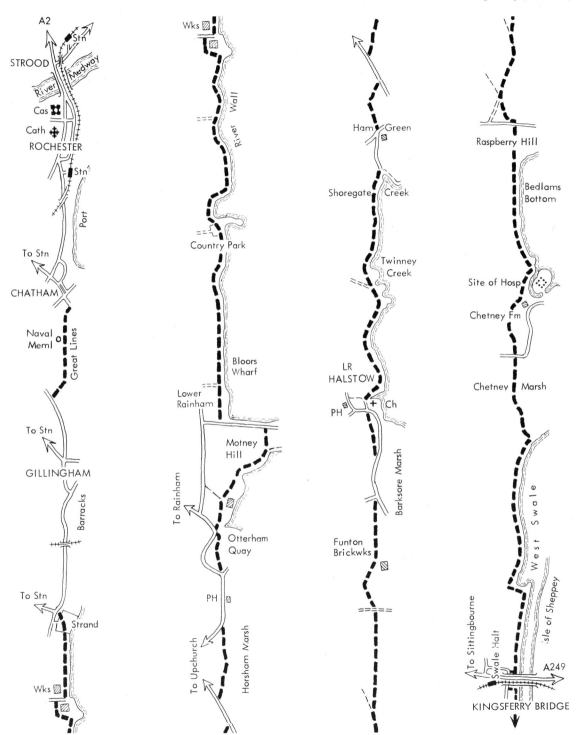

A2

Stn

STROOD

River Medway

Cas

Cath

ROCHESTER

Stn

Port

To Stn

CHATHAM

Naval Meml

Great Lines

To Stn

GILLINGHAM

Barracks

To Stn

Strand

Wks

Wks

River Wall

Country Park

Bloors Wharf

Lower Rainham

Motney Hill

To Rainham

Otterham Quay

PH

To Upchurch

Horsham Marsh

Ham Green

Shoregate Creek

Twinney Creek

LR HALSTOW

PH   Ch

Barksore Marsh

Funton Brickwks

Raspberry Hill

Bedlams Bottom

Site of Hosp

Chetney Fm

Chetney Marsh

West Swale

Isle of Sheppey

To Sittingbourne

Swale Halt

A249

KINGSFERRY BRIDGE

DAY 3: Kingsferry–Faversham (20 miles)

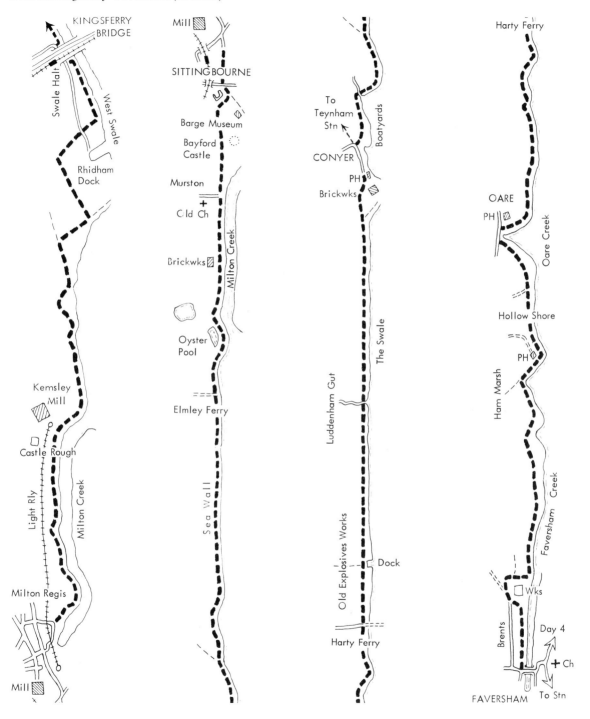

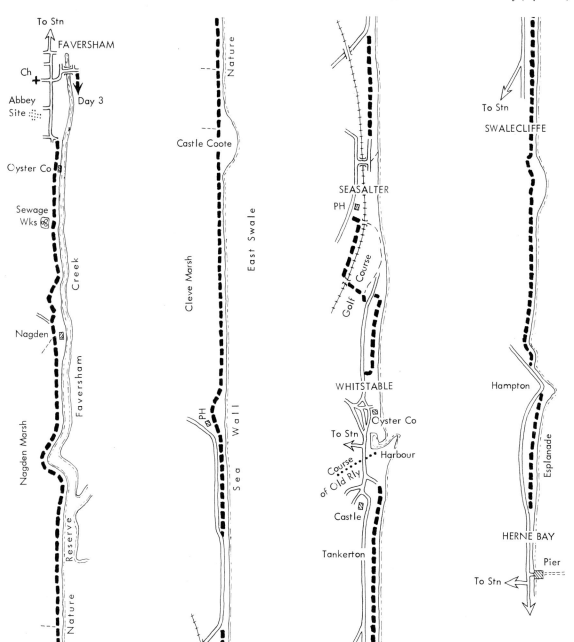

To Stn

FAVERSHAM

Ch

Abbey
Site

Day 3

Oyster Co

Sewage
Wks

Creek

Nagden

Faversham

Nagden Marsh

Reserve

Nature

Nature

Castle Coote

Cleve Marsh

East Swale

Sea Wall

PH

SEASALTER

PH

Golf Course

WHITSTABLE

Oyster Co

To Stn

Harbour

Course
of Old Rly

Castle

Tankerton

To Stn

SWALECLIFFE

Hampton

Esplanade

HERNE BAY

Pier

To Stn

DAY 5: Herne Bay–Sandwich (18 miles)

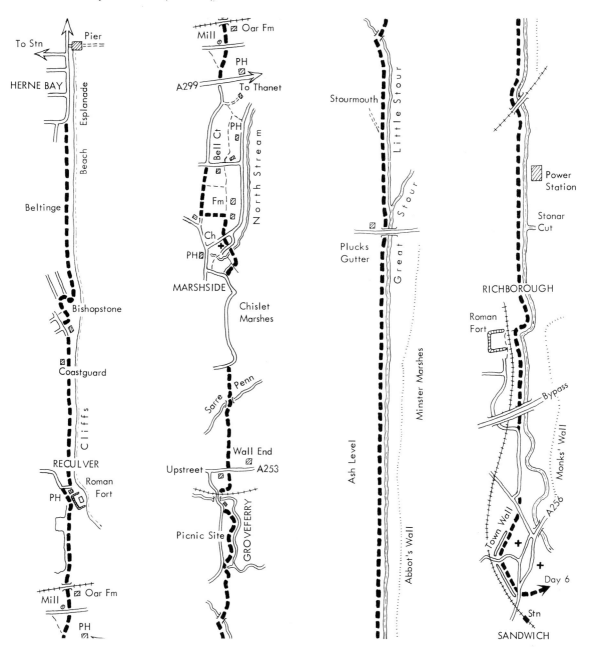

To Stn

Pier

HERNE BAY

Esplanade

Beach

Beltinge

Bishopstone

Coastguard

Cliffs

RECULVER

Roman Fort

PH

Mill
Oar Fm
PH

Mill
Oar Fm
A299
PH
To Thanet

Bell Ct

PH

Fm
North Stream

Ch
PH

MARSHSIDE

Chislet Marshes

Sarre Penn

Wall End
Upstreet
A253

GROVE FERRY

Picnic Site

Stourmouth

Little Stour

Stour

Plucks Gutter

Great Stour

Ash Level

Minster Marshes

Abbot's Wall

Power Station

Stonar Cut

RICHBOROUGH

Roman Fort

Bypass

Monks' Wall

A256

Town Wall

Day 6

Stn
SANDWICH

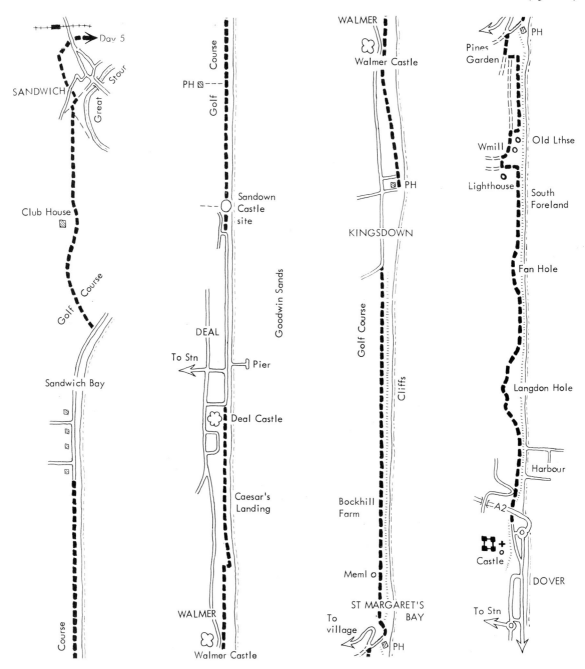

Day 5

SANDWICH

Great Stour

Club House

Golf Course

Sandwich Bay

Course

Golf Course

PH

Sandown Castle site

Goodwin Sands

DEAL

To Stn

Pier

Deal Castle

Caesar's Landing

WALMER

Walmer Castle

WALMER

Walmer Castle

PH

KINGSDOWN

Golf Course

Cliffs

Bockhill Farm

Meml

ST MARGARET'S BAY

To village

PH

Pines Garden

PH

Wmill

Old Lthse

Lighthouse

South Foreland

Fan Hole

Langdon Hole

Harbour

A2

Castle

DOVER

To Stn

DAY 7: Dover–Hythe (Downs route, 13 miles)/Sandling (15 miles)

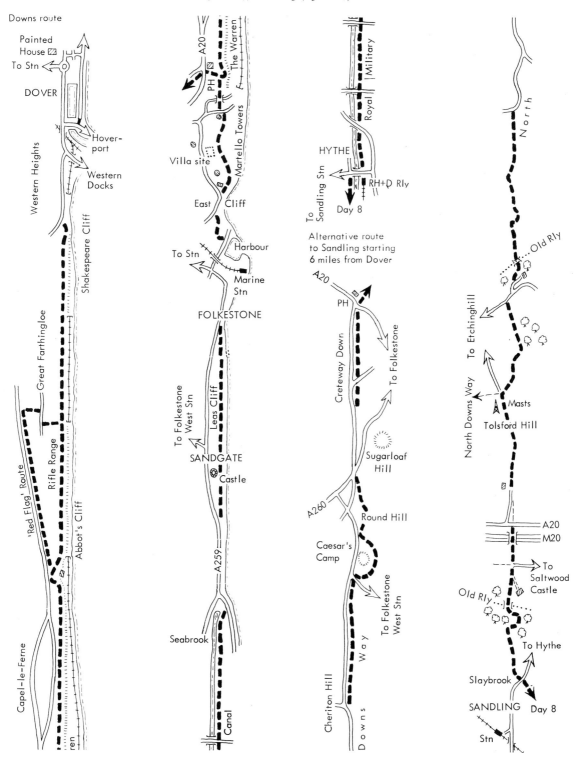

Downs route

Painted House
To Stn
DOVER
Western Heights
Hoverport
Western Docks
Shakespeare Cliff
Great Farthingloe
'Red Flag' Route
Rifle Range
Abbot's Cliff
Capel-le-Ferne
ren

A20
The Warren
PH
Villa site
Martello Towers
East Cliff
Harbour
To Stn
Marine Stn
FOLKESTONE
To Folkestone West Stn
Leas Cliff
SANDGATE
Castle
A259
Seabrook
Canal

Royal Military
HYTHE
To Sandling Stn
RH+D Rly
Day 8

Alternative route to Sandling starting 6 miles from Dover

A20
PH
Creteway Down
To Folkestone
Sugarloaf Hill
A260
Round Hill
Caesar's Camp
To Folkestone West Stn
Cheriton Hill
Downs Way

North
Old Rly
To Etchinghill
North Downs Way
Masts
Tolsford Hill
A20
M20
To Saltwood Castle
Old Rly
To Hythe
Slaybrook
SANDLING   Day 8
Stn

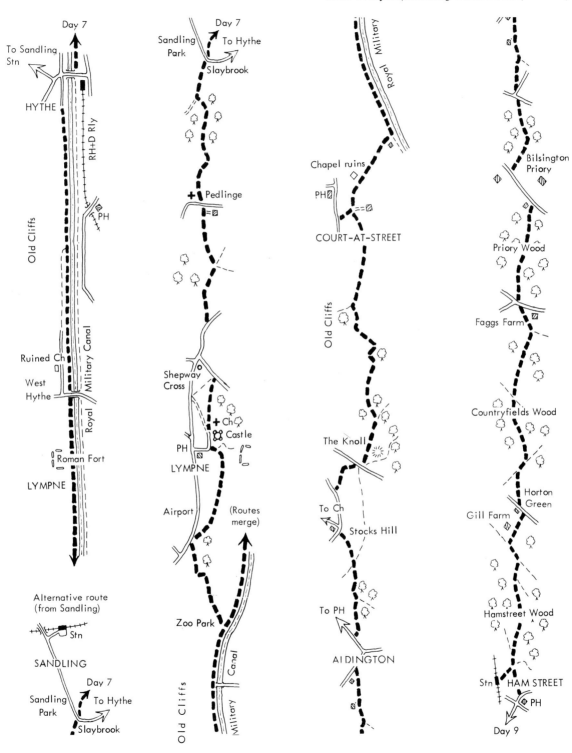

DAY 9: Ham Street–Rye (12 miles)

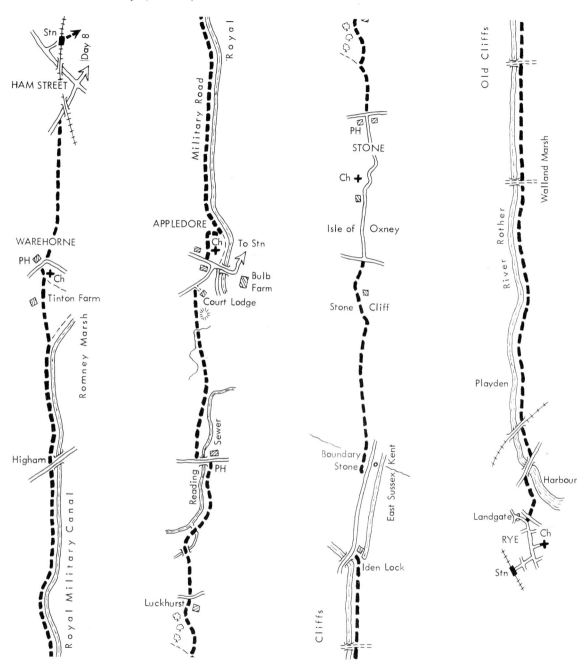

Stn

Day 8

HAM STREET

WAREHORNE

PH

Ch

Tinton Farm

Higham

Romney Marsh

Royal Military Canal

Military Road

Royal

APPLEDORE

Ch   To Stn

Bulb Farm

Court Lodge

Sewer

Reading

PH

Luckhurst

PH

STONE

Ch

Isle of   Oxney

Stone   Cliff

Boundary Stone

East Sussex/Kent

Iden Lock

Cliffs

Old Cliffs

River Rother

Walland Marsh

Playden

Harbour

Landgate

Ch

RYE

Stn

Index